MAKE
A MOVE

MAKE A MOVE

How to **Stop Wavering** and **Make Decisions** in a Disorienting World

Stephanie Williams O'Brien

Broadleaf Books
Minneapolis

CONTENTS

In memory of my father,
who instilled in me
a desire for
God's wisdom and
discernment.
Robert L. Williams, 1949–2000

PART 1

DISCERNMENT THROUGH MOVEMENT

Do not be too timid and squeamish about your actions. All life is an experiment. The more experiments you make the better. What if they are a little coarse and you may get your coat soiled or torn? What if you do fail, and get fairly rolled in the dirt once or twice? Up again, you shall never be so afraid of a tumble.

—Ralph Waldo Emerson

1

ALL LIFE IS AN EXPERIMENT

I sat alone in an empty house hundreds of miles from home. I could feel my heartbeat pick up the pace as though I were jogging and beginning to sprint. Beads of sweat gathered on my forehead, I started to feel light-headed, and I thought I was going to faint, or be sick, or both. I tried to take a deep breath, but it was as though someone had shrunk my lungs to half their capacity, and I couldn't get the oxygen in quickly enough.

"What should I do? What should I do?" The refrain circled in my brain, and I couldn't get it to stop. Soon it came pouring loudly out of my mouth and into the small room along with my tears.

I look back on that experience from a handful of years ago and realize that the unfamiliar set of sensations was a panic attack. I had experienced anxiety in my life before, but nothing like that. I felt completely out of control.

What was it that brought on one of the most intense experiences of my life?

A decision.

Research suggests we make up to thirty-five thousand decisions a day—from what we will wear and eat, to how we respond to others, to which route we will take to work.[1] But then there are decisions like the one I was facing—decisions you know will be life-altering depending on which option you choose. It was one of those deep, "this changes everything" decisions that caused my first panic attack.

Those sort of life-altering decisions don't come around every day. However, many of the decisions I face daily are important enough that they raise my blood pressure or shoot some amount of cortisol through my body. We make the majority of our thirty-five thousand decisions each day without thinking about it. But how do we approach the ones that are more important and consequential?

As I began to regain control of my mind and heart following that scary panic attack, I realized why this decision had shaken me to the core. I simply didn't know what to do in a scenario that would be life-altering no matter the outcome. I had tried everything: making lists of pros and cons, getting advice (advice that I was only *sometimes* actually asking for), and pleading with God to put "writing on the wall" or on some paper—*or really anywhere would be fine, God! Just tell me what to do!*

I tried every formula for decision-making I could find, and the only result was wavering that led me to severe decision paralysis. In the time since, I've had countless conversations with others about decision-making, and I always ask them this question: What is your philosophy of decision-making and spiritual discernment? Almost no one has a confident answer. That lack of a solid approach to making important decisions in life can hold us back and keep us wavering when we may otherwise make a move and take bold steps—even when the future is uncertain.

If I review the story of my life, I see many moments like this, where I felt tortured by a decision—not to the point of full-out panic, but tortured nevertheless. An unavoidable aspect of the human experience is that we will face many truly life-changing decisions. And many of our decisions affect others significantly.

What I didn't fully realize in that moment is that I wasn't alone in my decision-making. *Something* tells us, as people trying to follow God in this world, that the decisions are about more than just us or our lists of pros and cons. That *something* is the Holy Spirit.

One of the last things Jesus said to his closest friends on earth was that they would never be alone. That he was going to send the Spirit to be with them.[2] He said that the Holy Spirit would be a "counselor." The word in Greek is *parakletos*. It is sometimes translated as "helper, advocate, or comforter."

Jesus wanted his friends to understand how important this Spirit truly is because he stayed on the subject for quite a while. He said the Spirit is your helper and will always be with you and never leave you. This counselor will help you remember all that Jesus said but will also help teach you what you have yet to learn. The Spirit advocates for truth—the truth about who you are, your deepest identity, in light of the truth about God and God's identity.

While I admit this all sounds a lot more mystical than a pros-and-cons list, I think I like it. In that moment of panic, I would have loved a helper or a comforter. A counselor to help untangle the thoughts in my mind and the emotions that seemed to be attacking my heart. But all I could actually ask for in that moment was an answer. Not a guide, not an advocate of truth, but an "I'm freaking out here, so just tell me what to do!"

My understanding of God for much of my life had not led me to an encounter with the Spirit of God; rather, it had taught me that I should be asking God to just tell me the *right* answer. In hindsight, I can see that the decisions I made were rarely "right or wrong" but rather "bad, OK, good, better, or best." They were less about God having one specific will for the situation and more about God offering a counselor who would help me wrestle through the decisions that didn't have a clear right or wrong answer.

NOT MERELY A WILL BUT A WAY

Our obsession with the "will of God" is well documented. Many preachers, scholars, and pastors have argued that the pursuit of the will of God is encouraged throughout Scripture, and I wouldn't disagree. But when it comes to actually determining the will of God, I think we run into a methodological problem.

A select few stories in the Bible lead us to believe that God will show up with clear answers—stories of God audibly speaking, waking up a sleeping person, showing up in a flaming bush, writing on a wall with a creepy floating hand, or some equally disturbing image.

God could, and may still, speak this way to some people in some instances—I have no interest in limiting what God *can* do. But *most* of what we read in Scripture suggests that the way most followers of Yahweh have tried to figure out how God is leading is a lot messier and much less clear. Far more often, we see people in Scripture crying out to God for wisdom in the midst of complex situations rather than simply hearing God's voice.

When Jesus was speaking to his friends, he promised that this counselor would come after him. So they waited for the Spirit to come, and when it did, it was the fire that ignited what became the early church. If you follow their story through Acts, you'll see no burning bushes or creepy hands writing on walls. There were a few dreams and visions. But what seems most common is some sort of group brainstorming—or even bickering—and then a lot of what seems like trial and error.

But what if there is no such thing as trial and error?

THE SCIENTIFIC METHOD

A scientist would never consider their work "trial and error." They would say they are executing experiments and then learning from the results. Sure, there are times when an experiment is botched because the petri dish got contaminated. Or perhaps someone accidentally poured out the mason jar in which their little seahorses were going to hatch (I'm still getting over that one!).

These obvious mistakes aside, the point of an experiment is to learn and then to take what you learned into the next experiment. So an experiment isn't trial and *error*; it's trial and *learn*! The details of the scientific method vary depending on whom you ask, but the steps are relatively simple:

Step 1: Define your question—or what you are hoping to learn.

Step 2: Do your research and creative brainstorming—see what has been learned and what answers have been discovered by others in the past. Also make sure you consider various creative options for the experiment itself.

Step 3: Determine the first experiment you will try that will answer your question or help you learn more.

Step 4: Name the steps of your experiment and execute them for a predetermined amount of time.

Step 5: Analyze and review the results and determine what was learned.

When I read about the encounters Jesus's early followers had with the counselor, the helper we call the Holy Spirit, they appear to be following something like the scientific method. When something that seems supernatural does happen, they aren't usually waiting for it. Rather, they keep their eyes and ears open as they are on the move. It is in the midst of these experiments that they notice different ways God's Spirit is leading. But they don't seem to be digging for the "will of God" each time they encounter a new decision.

Rather, it seems more like a series of experiments takes them to places they never would have planned to visit before they set off. Imagine if they had hosted a "strategic planning meeting" before launching arguably the largest movement that humanity has ever witnessed. There is no doubt in my mind that their "strategic plan" would have paled in comparison to what God led—and is still leading—in this movement we call *the church*.

When it comes to the "will of God," we must ask, What if God is more interested in the *way* we make decisions than in the final decisions themselves?

Depending on your background, that question may be difficult to read. Hear me out on this. God seems much more interested in a relationship with humans than in forcing rituals onto them. The Spirit of God invites humans to join in God's work rather than be controlled and forced to do God's work.

When Jesus promised this counselor would come, he said to his friends, "Be careful to do everything I taught you." He wasn't talking to hear himself think out loud! However, it's clear that these aren't empty marching orders; rather, they are an invitation to a relationship where the Spirit will reveal God's preferred future—if that's what we actually *want* to see. To paraphrase Jesus in this part of the story, "Try to do everything I told you, but don't worry, I am going to send my Spirit to guide you because life is complex. If my leadership is truly what you want to seek, then the Spirit will lead you through the messiness of life."

Discernment for the Jesus follower is all about the relationship, not about getting it right or wrong. Perhaps the initial question we all need to ask is this: Do we want God's Spirit involved in our decisions? How we answer will determine the steps we will take. If we choose to approach life's decisions by creating experiments, they can give us an opportunity to see what is "good to us and the Holy Spirit," as the early church seems to wonder as they wander through their story.[3]

By the end of the first part of this book, you will see how each step of the scientific method involves God's leadership. But that's a good moment to stop and reflect on our openness to that leadership in the first place.

THE WAY, THE TRUTH, THE LIFE

While I think God rarely has one very specific will for each decision we need to make, God does want us to take steps of faith in order to join in what God is doing in the world around us and in our lives. This is a daily, moment-by-moment choice to be consciously dependent on the Holy Spirit in our everyday lives.

Does that mean some decisions aren't relegated to right or wrong or *in* God's will or *out* of God's will? Absolutely. Many, if not most, decisions involve more nuance and an invitation to use our own free will.

Jesus said to his friends, "I am the way and the truth and the life."⁴ Many followers of Jesus cling to this phrase as a source of identity. I think I know why: we so often don't know the way, we aren't sure what is true, and we know there has to be more to life. Jesus is saying that he is the way to God—yes, regarding our eternal future, but this phrase is about today and tomorrow as well.

If we want to make good decisions today—and if we want to avoid panic attacks tomorrow—we have to shift our mindset to recognize that many decisions don't have one perfect right answer that we must discover or else we've failed. In the experience I mentioned earlier, I was fixated on not getting this decision wrong, and that is what led to my crippling anxiety. It was not one of the more "resourced versions of myself," as my therapist has kindly defined. Demanding that God tell me what to do—as though there were only one specific will for my life in every situation—was not my best moment.

I was trying to get God to take the work of discernment off of my shoulders when I knew full well that God leading me around like a puppet on a string was not what I actually hoped for. I was not embracing the *full life* Jesus said⁵ he came to offer. Stay tuned for more on how this experience in my life unfolded.

Spiritual director Ruth Haley Barton defines *spiritual discernment* as "an ever increasing capacity to 'see' or discern the works of God in the midst of the human situation so that we can align ourselves with whatever God is doing."⁶ Being a part of what God is doing in the world will shape your decision-making in amazing ways.

I invite you to join me as we discover together the freedom, adventure, and strength that comes from asking Jesus to lead us in the *way* we make decisions. We can find great meaning in discerning God's leadership rather than begging for shortcuts and simplistic answers.

The beginning of this book will build on this framework for how we can think about decisions and discernment. Then in part 2, we will break down actual experiments that can help you stop wavering and make a move in various areas of your life. We will continue the book by talking about change—which is always a reality if we are going to make a move. Finally, we will wrap things up with tips on how to move into God's preferred future in your life from now on!

Together we will explore the idea that God's hope for us is less about a specific *will* and more about the lifelong pursuit of God's *way*.

2

NOT MERELY A WILL
BUT A WAY

How do I know God's will for my life?

How do I know where to go on life's journey?

You could have cut the tension in the room with a knife. My husband and I sat with our friends as they discussed the impasse they had come to in their relationship. One felt ready to commit—well, at least on a good day. The other had conflicting desires. He had spent much of his life dreaming about living overseas, and he struggled to see how this relationship could coexist with his insatiable hope to leave the country as he had planned for years.

They were stuck.

"I think you need to make a move," I said. They both stared at me wide-eyed as the sentence hung in the air. I'm not sure what went through their heads in that moment, but I was picking up what they seemed to be laying down: "Um, hello? We are stuck; that is exactly what we do *not* feel like we can do right now."

I knew I couldn't let that sit in the room too long, so I continued: "Sitting here talking in circles is not going to get you any closer to making a decision about your future together. You need to design an experiment that helps you learn more than you know now as you sit here in decision paralysis. You *can* make some moves that aren't as permanent like getting married or moving to the other side of the world! Perhaps taking some steps can help you discern what you are supposed to do long term."

We then brainstormed a few experiments they could try that would help them learn more than they knew now. These included taking a trip abroad together to see what that experience was like as well as some preengagement counseling to talk through how they make decisions together. They outlined the five steps mentioned in chapter 1 and started to get unstuck one move at a time.

Sure, it took time and even a financial investment. But discerning who you will join your life to through a covenant is one of the most important decisions you will make in your life—well worth a few experiments. Now, a couple years and many experiments later, they are married and planning to move overseas together.

People often think of discernment, especially spiritual discernment, as something to sit still and wait for, and they listen intently, hoping to hear something. I picture my springer spaniel cocking his head to the side and listening for something that is only audible to his canine ears. As I said, God *can* and *does* speak through quiet moments of stillness. I will always advocate for time away to listen. But there is absolutely more than one tool on the discernment tool bench.

Acts is a great place for us to learn how to engage with God's Spirit when it comes to trying to make decisions. These are the stories of the first folks trying to become the church and follow

Jesus after the Counselor, the Spirit, has been given to them. Reading these stories makes one thing very clear: following God is not clear-cut at all.

DISCERNMENT THROUGH MOVEMENT

We often refer to Acts as the "acts of the apostles," but I prefer to think of it as the "acts of the Holy Spirit." The story shows the Spirit leading the early church leaders, the apostles, and directing them where to go and what to do. In Acts, God often speaks to individuals directly during times of prayer but also by sending other people. The Spirit can speak in the stillness but also along the way. God's leadership usually invites people to make a move without giving them the whole picture. In fact, sometimes God gives an inaccurate picture of the future, but it still provides direction.

In the back of most Bibles is a little section of maps. Typically, one is called "Paul's Missionary Journeys." Paul was an early leader of the church in the first century. When I was a kid, I would get bored during the sermon, open to the back of the Bible, and trace my finger along the brightly colored lines that showed the direction of Paul's journey.

No wonder that when I became an adult, I subconsciously thought God would give me some sort of map with predetermined lines on it. I would then have to follow the lines journey by journey through my life. That sounds great, right? But when we read how these biblical journeys *actually* were discerned, we get a window into a very different picture than those shown in the orange and red lines on the maps in my NIV Bible.

Toward the middle of Acts, a group led by Paul was having trouble discerning where they should go. They traveled through what was then called the province of Asia, and the text says that the Holy Spirit prevented them from performing any ministry during that time.[1] They traveled at least a hundred miles only to find out they couldn't do what they had set out to do. I have had the experience of feeling held back from what I thought I was supposed to be doing—it's frustrating!

They came to the border of the province of Asia where it meets the province of Bithynia. Since they couldn't do anything in Asia, they figured that perhaps if they crossed over into Bithynia, they could continue their work. Nope. The Scripture says, "The Spirit of Jesus would not allow them to."[2]

Now, I wish there was more explanation here. Did they have some internal sense of unease or a lack of peace about crossing the border? Or did Jesus pull a Princess Leia and appear by holo-gram, saying, "I will not allow you to cross"? Well, it doesn't tell us exactly what happened, so I choose to imagine a Star Wars hologram. Obviously.

God led them not by telling them what to do but rather by tell-ing them what *not* to do. And notice that they didn't sit still and pout when a door seemed to close. (And no offense to the cliché, but it doesn't seem like any windows were opening either.) They just kept going. Traveling another hundred miles from the border of Asia and Bithynia, they finally made it to a city called Troas, a port on the coast of the Aegean Sea.

Finally, that night, they received a sign from God that seemed to suggest God's will for what they should actually *do* rather than not do. This resonates with me so deeply. I've never trav-eled by foot or caravan two hundred miles with nothing but closed doors. But I have experienced doors closing in my face when opportunities that seemed good and maybe even right were shut down. And I haven't seen a hologram of Jesus—or Princess Leia or Obi-Wan Kenobi, for that matter—telling me what to do or what not do. But I have felt like I was walking for days on end, not knowing if I was even going in the right direction for my life.

Paul had a dream that a man from a region across the sea in Macedonia was asking for help: "Help us, Paul of Tarsus; you're our only hope!" Couldn't resist that one.

He woke everyone up in the middle of the night so they could get on the first boat across the sea to Macedonia. It might seem rude to make the whole team leave in a rush, but after hundreds of miles of dead ends, I think I would have done the same.

They got across the sea, but no one was waiting there for help, so they moved from town to town. Then they did something that is a pattern throughout the lives of these first Jesus followers—they found a place to pray. It was the time of day they typically stopped to listen and talk to God. It was also the Sabbath and would have been a day they focused on God even more intently.

Those of us whose religious traditions don't instruct us to pray at specific times each day might assume that this would lead to a rote or stiff relationship with God. Sometimes people worry that strict prayer rituals are inauthentic because there are many days you might not feel like praying or listening. For the Jews and early Christians we read about in Acts (as well as for many devoutly religious people today), scheduled prayer times aren't the only time God leads, but they sure are an important part of the equation. I'm sure that, more often than not, when Paul and the others practiced their daily prayers, nothing supernatural happened. But on this day, when they stopped and took time to pray, it led them to an influential woman in the fashion industry. You'll see . . .

Paul and his friends went to a river outside the city gate in Philippi to what they heard was a place of prayer. A group of women were there, so they began to talk with them about Jesus. Lydia, who was likely a successful businesswoman in fashion, was among them. God opened Lydia's heart, and she and her whole household were baptized.

In the culture of the ancient Near East, where Paul and Lydia are situated in history, a *household* (*oikos* in Greek) is not what we would imagine today. Rather than a nuclear family or even an extended family group related by blood, an *oikos* was an economic grouping of people, many of whom probably lived on Lydia's compound, which had multiple dwellings. So this was a significant group of people—likely from a more elite part of society—becoming Jesus followers.

So the "man from Macedonia" in Paul's dream ended up being a woman in the fashion industry. I'm not sure why God didn't just give Paul a dream about Lydia. My hunch is that if Paul tried to wake up his buddies in the middle of the night to start packing because he had a dream about a rich lady across the sea beckoning for him to help, they would have rolled their eyes and gone back to sleep.

My friend Jo talks about how Lydia is the "gateway" for the gospel's journey to Europe[3] because Lydia is the first Jesus follower in the European region. The church that started in Philippi out of her home/compound flourished. It's easy to see how Lydia's resources and partnership were critical in its success and the spread of Christianity throughout Europe from there.

In the end, many men from Macedonia were helped through the ministry that Lydia started, so perhaps the vision wasn't completely incorrect. But Paul could have easily missed what God was doing right in front of him if he had been too fixated on only the vision. Paul and his group had become familiar with what I call "discernment through movement." When they didn't hear anything from God, they kept moving. When they saw what seemed like God, they made a move toward it with their eyes wide open along the way, knowing that God's Spirit was constantly moving.

TAKING NOTES FROM PAUL, LYDIA, AND FRIENDS

While our stories may look nothing like those of Paul and his friends or Lydia and her household, we can glean some principles for following the Spirit and making decisions even when we aren't sure of the next step.

First of all, we can accept that there isn't a road map for life. It seems obvious, but I find myself acting like one will eventually appear in my glove compartment out of nowhere. As soon as we let go of the idea that no one is going to give us a map—not even God—we can move on to wondering how we should expect to experience God's guidance.

Next, we can realize that it's normal for doors to close. It's normal to find ourselves in a spot where we don't get to do what we set out to do. I love starting things—I'm a strange pastor version of a serial entrepreneur. Because of this, I've had a lot of experiences where I thought I was going to start something awesome just to feel like the door got slammed in my face. These "closed doors" and "dead ends" can lead us in the right direction, if we let them. The key is to keep moving. I don't know how many times I've seen people hit a dead end and sit down and pout, frustrated with where they ended up. Sure, it's frustrating, and we may even need to sulk a little bit. But we don't need to stay there. Paul and company kept on going, keeping their eyes and ears open for the next step.

In this story, we see that the Holy Spirit will interrupt at the most unexpected times—like when Paul had a vision in the middle of the night. At the same time, the Spirit also gets our attention when we are showing up for the very purpose of communing with God. Lydia was at a place of prayer. As I mentioned, we can choose to make space in our lives on the regular to connect with God. Many times it can seem uneventful or, if we are honest, like God isn't even there! But what about the times when God may want to introduce us to something potentially life-changing? How many times had Lydia chosen to show up to pray before this encounter that shifted the trajectory of her life so significantly that we are talking about her thousands of years later? She's been an inspiration to so many—my friend even named her little girl after her!

Finally, in this story, we see that sometimes we really have our sights set on something—like a vision of what we have set out to do—but in the end, discernment through movement leads us to something completely different. Paul had a vision of a man asking for help, but he trusted the Spirit in his encounter with Lydia. He could have said, "Sorry, lady. We can't be bothered to come to your home. We saw a vision of a man, so we have to wait until we see that vision come to fruition." But he didn't. God often gives us a picture or an idea that helps us begin to move. We may not start moving in the middle of the night like Paul did, but these nudges from God can help get us going. Instead of thinking of a vision or a hope or a nudge as some sort of fortune-telling about the future, we can see that God was just moving Paul in the right direction so that God could do something Paul would *never* have dreamed of!

Let's see how this story fits into the framework for experimenting I mentioned in the previous chapter.

With some creative license, here is what I think Paul would say. If Paul were to start with step 1, he would define his question like this: "Where does God want us to go next on our journey to share about freedom in Jesus?"

This wasn't his first rodeo, so in step 2, the "research" was all those experiences from the past when they moved from place to place, keeping their eyes open, and God led them to discern through movement.

Step 3 is where you determine your experiment. From what we know about Paul's journeys, he and his companions often wondered together what God might lead them to try next.

God used other people to lead them as well, so I imagine that in step 4, they made plans and outlined their steps for action: to keep moving, with their eyes peeled and their ears perked, and take it one day at a time.

We don't know for sure, but I bet they had many conversations on the road as they tried to decipher what seemed good to them and the Holy Spirit. When we look at the whole story of Paul and his journeys, we can tell that they must have engaged in step 5, analyzing and reviewing the results in order to determine what they learned. I don't think they wasted an ounce of what they discovered from experiment to experiment. Now here we are thousands of years later, analyzing their results and seeing what we can learn as well.

Many decisions we face in our lives are not too complex, but then we have those where a lot is at stake. When this is the case, you can make a move by designing an experiment that will help you learn more than you know now. Instead of a "trial and error" approach, think "experiment and learn." When life doesn't give you a map with bright-colored lines to follow, then perhaps, like Paul and company, you'll find your path as you are actually walking on it. I personally have never seen God, or a burning bush, or a hologram claiming to be divine. I've also never heard God's audible voice, but I have sensed God, seen what God is doing, and felt distinctly that God put words and pictures in my mind and my heart to lead me.

In the next chapter, we will discuss what hearing from God can look like in our lives if it is indeed not an audible voice. But let me leave you with this simple prayer that I pray every day: "God, open my eyes to what you are doing around me. Attune my ears to your voice, and give me the courage to respond and follow you to the best of my ability."

3

INVITATIONS LEFT UNOPENED

Why would God speak to me?

How can I be certain that what I hear is from God?

Junk mail nearly ruined one of my friendships.

I get so much junk mail each week. I try to recycle it daily and separate out the mail I actually want to read, but I inevitably wind up with a pile of unsorted mail for a week or sometimes even two. This has caused more than a couple of issues when I miss a bill or fail to see that a piece of mail requires a timely response.

But the worst junk mail fail was when I sorted through the mail and ended up leaving the invitation to my friend's wedding unopened in a pile. I didn't realize it was there! I assumed I wasn't invited or had been forgotten, and bitterness began to take root. My friend, on the other hand, had begun to wonder why I was so rude not to RSVP to one of the most important events of her life. An awkward text conversation revealed my error, and the friendship was saved.

We live in a time of communication overload. Of course, an abundance of snail mail is only the beginning. We are inundated daily with emails, texts, and digital messages through countless apps. I'm left wondering how often we may not be getting the messages and invitations we actually want to receive.

Our communication overload even causes us to miss out on God's invitations for us in our daily lives. Jesus is inviting us to join him in what he is doing in the world around us. The Spirit of God is inviting us to see ourselves and others differently. God is inviting us to see the beauty all around us, even in tragedy. But these invitations are piling up in our minds and hearts and getting stuck in the junk filters of life.

So what if we started to intentionally look for the invitations from God all around us? Perhaps some are left unopened that could reveal God's heart for us as we discern the moves to make in our lives. Maybe God has already been trying to get our attention in one area of life while we were begging for God to guide us in a whole other aspect.

God is not like me or my friend. God has so much more patience. God often sends invitations more than once in order to make sure we don't assume we are not invited in the first place. You may be reading this and feeling like God hasn't sent you any invitations lately. Let's explore a few reasons you might be feeling that way.

"I'M NOT WORTHY" AND OTHER SNEAKY TEMPTATIONS

I think very little about my financial "worth" as a person in the world. I try to save some money each month and pay off my credit cards, but that's about it. Something I *do* think about often is my worthiness. It can be tempting to believe that we are not worthy of what God offers us for our lives.

Why would God speak to me? What do I have to offer anyway? I'm not like those in the Bible whom God spoke to; they had special worth to God. If you have been hearing these sneaky lies of unworthiness, remember just how freely God offered leadership to the characters in Scripture who were not as special as they might have seemed on the surface. They were ordinary and broken people just like you and me. You see God speaking to people like Abraham and Sarah, who had major trust issues. You watch God use people like Moses with his major confidence issues and Rahab, David, and Matthew, who all had some very questionable morals.

On one hand, it's true that none of us are worthy of the God of the universe speaking and leading us. This is central to the Christian faith, that God chooses to make us worthy by adopting us into God's family. According to Jesus, we are even *worth* dying for! God chose to give us worth through Jesus. Jesus took to the cross all the unworthiness that comes from our inability to live the life God intended for us before brokenness entered and fractured the world.

Jesus's message "I am the way and the truth and the life" offers the promise that he is in the restoration business, bringing new life, healing, and wholeness to all that is fractured. If we want to accept the invitation, we can join that mission and live in that way. This renewal is happening all around us if we are paying attention.

So it makes sense that we sometimes feel unworthy to be spoken to and led by the God of the universe. But as followers of Jesus, by embracing all that he went through to prove our worth, we can see how incredibly worthy Jesus invites us to become!

If you feel like you haven't been receiving invitations from God in your life to join in what God is doing in the world, I encourage you to embrace the worthiness that Jesus offers to whoever wants it.

THE TWELVE STEPS ARE FOR EVERYONE

Once I was in a serious dating relationship with someone while he got sober for the first time after fifteen years of being a high-functioning alcoholic who kept his drinking a secret from me and everyone else in his life. Finding out that someone I've never seen touch a drink was drinking daily in secret is one of the most difficult experiences of my life; watching someone step into sobriety is one of the most amazing.

During that season, Alcoholics Anonymous (AA) became an important part of his life, as it has been for many. And Al-Anon became an important part of my life. If you aren't familiar with it, Al-Anon is a recovery group for the families and friends of alcoholics, whether or not the alcoholic recognizes the existence of a drinking problem.

To pursue peace while trying to support an alcoholic is very difficult. One of the most common mistakes is thinking that you can't have peace unless your loved one has peace—as though your peace depends on them. But as AA teaches, we can only have peace if we first accept it from God.

Al-Anon taught me what I had learned many different times in different ways throughout my life as a Jesus follower. We all must answer one question before we can experience peace from God and truly discern God's invitations in our lives: Will I surrender my life to God?

Some of you may know the first three steps of the twelve steps of AA:[1]

1. We admitted we were powerless over alcohol—that our lives had become unmanageable.
2. Came to believe that a Power greater than ourselves could restore us to sanity.

3. Made a decision to turn our will and our lives over to the care of God as we understood God.

In the AA community, there is a concept called "the gift of desperation." Those who experience desperation can realize that their lives are unmanageable on their own. In reality, all of our lives are unmanageable on our own, but those who struggle with addiction have often hit the end of their rope and are desperate—and that leads them to truly surrender. It's a gift because surrender is the first step to experiencing God's peace, and it also leads us to the foundation of the discernment of everything else in our lives.

One of the reasons many feel as though God is not offering them invitations in their lives is because they have not surrendered to God. In some ways, surrender is the mailbox placed out front, ready to receive the invitations God wants to send. Some of us have our proverbial mailbox hidden or buried. Perhaps we didn't realize this was true, or we knew we buried it because it's risky to tell the God of the universe that you are open to God's invitations. They aren't always safe, but they are always good.

CERTAINTY VERSUS ASSURANCE

In my book *Stay Curious: How Questions and Doubts Can Save Your Faith*, I wrote about how true certainty is a myth and unattainable. I wrote that book because I realized how much we struggle as humans with the desire for certainty and our lack of it. Certainty when it comes to decision-making is knowing for sure that we have made the *right* decision. Certainty is getting a chance to see the outcomes of our decisions before we take the risk and make a move. Certainty is wanting to know for sure that we are hearing God accurately. God doesn't invite us into a life of certainty but rather a life of assurance.

The assurance offered by God means that we are never alone; God is with us. The Holy Spirit is with us no matter what decision we make. No matter where our decisions fall on the spectrum from bad to OK and from good to great, God will be with us throughout and on the other end of the decision.

God's assurance invites us to trust the Holy Spirit and accept that all we can do is our best.

God's assurance means that we can have peace in the midst of the many aspects of life that are not within our control.

God's assurance allows God's love to motivate us to make decisions that increasingly reflect the heart that God has for us, others, and the world.

One of the most important tools of AA is the Serenity Prayer. The original version was written by Reinhold Niebuhr, a pastor who died in the 1970s. Today, this shortened version has become the most memorized and recited today:

> God, give me grace to accept with serenity
> the things that cannot be changed,
> Courage to change the things
> which should be changed,
> and the wisdom to distinguish
> the one from the other.

The word *serenity* is typically defined as the state of being calm, peaceful, and untroubled. So at the risk of making an unwanted edit to this important prayer, I often encourage people to read it with the word *peace* instead of *serenity*, since that is a more common word in our world today:

God, give me grace to accept with [peace]
the things that cannot be changed,
Courage to change the things
which should be changed,
and the wisdom to distinguish
the one from the other.

But there is more to Pastor Niebuhr's prayer that is not as familiar to most:

Living one day at a time,
Enjoying one moment at a time,
Accepting hardship as a pathway to peace,
Taking, as Jesus did,
This sinful world as it is,
Not as I would have it,
Trusting that You will make all things right,
If I surrender to Your will,
So that I may be reasonably happy in this life,
And supremely happy with You forever in the next. Amen.

As I began to calm down from the aforementioned panic attack of 2015 (as I have come to refer to it in my own mind), I looked around the room for what could comfort me. I was alone, sitting in the living room of the man whom I was seriously dating at the time. He was just a few months away from his two years of sobriety. As I said, it was incredible to watch him go through that powerful experience. But we were nearing a crossroads where the healing he had experienced didn't seem to be enough to hold the relationship together.

I didn't know what to do—stay with the man I loved and with whom I had been through so much or let him go, trusting that

God needed to use that relational space in his life to bring further healing.

I wiped the tears from my eyes and tried to slow down my breathing. As my blurred vision became focused again, I saw the small plaque on the wall, took a deep breath, and began to read it out loud as many times as I needed to until my heart rate slowed to normal:

> God, give me grace to accept with serenity
> the things that cannot be changed,
> Courage to change the things
> which should be changed,
> and the wisdom to distinguish
> the one from the other.

4

IS SEEING BELIEVING?

Do I truly want to hear from God?

What does the Holy Spirit's leading really look like?

There are two types of people in this world: those who are OK with little notification bubbles with numbers climbing into the double digits and those who *must* clear those notifications in order to remain sane. I am the second type of person.

Every once in a while, I get a glimpse of someone's phone or laptop with the little red bubbles full of unread notifications, and my mind starts to explode. Clearly, I am the one who needs to pull myself together, because the amount of information coming at us from all sides is not going to subside any time soon. Inevitably, things will need to go unread. The real struggle in life is the same struggle I had with physical junk mail: how to sort out the information in order to process it in ways that would help me move forward. Which notifications actually need my attention? Similarly, of everything around me, what does God want me to notice?

If somewhere among all the information moving toward us in the universe are invitations from God, then the true challenge is to determine what may be from God and what can be discarded. We each hear from God or see God move in vastly different ways. To provide a formula for what that may look, feel, or sound like would fail to acknowledge the complexity with which God chooses to interact with humans. However, exploring how others experience God's leadership can expand your own understanding and open you up to possibilities that may give you an awareness of God's movement around you!

SQUINTING FAITH

In the last chapter, we discussed how certainty is a myth, and all we can depend on is the assurance that God offers. Certainty and faith can't coexist—faith can be grounded in assurance, but not in certainty. On the road of life, it can be tempting to overcorrect away from the "ditch of certainty" and into the "ditch of blind faith." "Blind faith" is the idea that true faith means we cannot see what may be ahead, and thus we have to take steps forward, feeling our way along as though we were completely blind from a spiritual perspective.

Jesus has a lot to say about the metaphor of blindness.[1] In the Gospels, he heals people who are physically blind,[2] but he also makes a number of statements about the concept of spiritual blindness. He refers to himself as the light that shines in the darkness.[3] At one point, some religious leaders confronted Jesus for healing a blind man on the Sabbath, which their legalism prohibited. Jesus said, "I have come into this world, so that the blind will see and those who see will become blind."[4] Jesus is suggesting that the clarity the religious leaders thought they had, and the feeling of superiority over others that comes with it, is not truly seeing but rather a form of spiritual blindness.

What we don't want to miss is that Jesus is also suggesting you *can* see spiritually. Jesus often spoke in parables, or short stories that illustrated something he wanted to teach those who were listening. When asked why he spoke in parables, he answered by quoting Isaiah, a very famous prophet from the Old Testament whom everyone listening would have recognized. Here is what Jesus says in Matthew 13:13–16:

> This is why I speak to them in parables:
> "Though seeing, they do not see;
>> though hearing, they do not hear or understand.
>
> In them is fulfilled the prophecy of Isaiah:
> "'You will be ever hearing but never understanding;
>> you will be ever seeing but never perceiving.
> For this people's heart has become calloused;
>> they hardly hear with their ears,
>> and they have closed their eyes.
> Otherwise they might see with their eyes,
>> hear with their ears,
>> understand with their hearts
> and turn, and I would heal them.'
>
> But blessed are your eyes because they see, and your ears because they hear."

Jesus makes it clear that it is possible to see and hear what God is trying to say. He doesn't promise it will always be clear, but it's possible. So perhaps the best way to think about seeing God move is to say that we can have *squinting* faith.

I am significantly nearsighted. When I don't have my glasses on, I can't see clearly more than two or three inches in front of my face. But when I squint, at times I can make out the words on a sign in the distance. If I am in a familiar environment and I squint, I'm able to make it around pretty well despite how unclear and fuzzy much of the landscape appears to my naked eyes.

It's similar when we follow God's movement in our lives. We don't have to assume we have blind faith, but it's not twenty-twenty vision either. When we become familiar with looking for and responding to God, then some effort to squint and work hard to see through the blur, coupled with a growing familiarity with our relationship with God, can get us on the path of discernment even in difficult decisions. Remember that Paul came to faith through an experience of physical blindness to help him see his spiritual blindness.[5] Throughout the rest of the story we see in the book of Acts, Paul's faith deepened and his spiritual eyes were opened. Though he couldn't see the path clearly, he was able to keep one foot in front of the other and stay on the move following the Spirit.

That is, of course, if we actually want to see God move and hear God's voice.

TELLING OURSELVES WHAT WE WANT TO HEAR

Before we get into the specifics of the ways we can look at and listen to God, we all must reckon with one question: Is God's voice what I really want to hear?

There are times when we so deeply want direction in our lives, but we fail to realize the surrender involved in the process. Recall that first step of the twelve steps of Alcoholics Anonymous. If we want spiritual discernment from God, then we must explore within ourselves whether we are ready to hear from God. Are you ready to see God's movement and respond to God's invitations?

I don't want to gloss over the reality that it takes a significant amount of trust to listen and respond to God. Jesus invites his followers to trust him many times throughout the Gospels. I think that is because he knows it's difficult to do so. Whenever Jesus seems to repeat something, it's a good sign we need to pay close attention.

A reading through the Gospels may not immediately make it clear how often Jesus invites trust from those he is leading. The English translation for the word *pisteuo* is typically "believe." While that is not a bad translation for this Greek word, another translation would be "trust." In the Western world, we have come to equate the word *believe* with an intellectual agreement with a concept. With that definition, trusting Jesus is pretty different from believing in Jesus.

Let's swap "believe" with "trust" in some familiar sayings of Jesus from the Gospels:

"Do not be afraid, just trust me."[6]

"Do you trust me?"[7]

"Unless you see signs and wonders you won't trust me."[8]

The old adages "Seeing is believing" and "I'll believe it when I see it" presume that actual evidence is necessary for believing, that faith without proof and certainty is not an option.

What if it's more accurate to say, "Seeing is trusting"?

Perhaps to truly see what God is doing, the first step is trust.

Do you trust God's words enough to hear God's voice? Do you trust God's story enough to see God move?

It doesn't have to be perfect trust; there is no such thing. We may have to muster up what little trust we can find. We may need to exclaim to God what the man whose son needed healing said to Jesus: "I trust, help me overcome my distrust."[9]

There are many reasons we struggle to trust God. A short list might include people who say they represent God but cause abuse, hypocritical people who say they are faithful but act otherwise, the reality that God is not physically present, and feeling like prayers have gone unheard. All of these things and more can cause us to struggle to trust God. I have no desire to minimize these barriers, but I do see an invitation to do what we can to trust in the midst of them and even ask God to help us do so.

If God's voice is truly what we want to hear in our lives, then I propose two questions to ask daily that will center us in the leadership of God's Spirit every day:

1. God, what are you saying to me?
2. How do you want me to respond?

Even if we aren't sure what God is saying, as we listen, our posture can be that of someone ready to respond to what they may hear. Another way of stating question 2 is "What am I going to do about it?"

If we think God is trying to get our attention in some way, then we need to be ready so that guidance can make a significant difference in every area of our lives. Following Jesus then becomes a practice of listening and responding rather than some sort of list of right or wrong or merely a moral code.

As I have encouraged people to follow Jesus in this way, as in intentional and intimate daily response to the Spirit, some have described the experience as almost like coming to faith again for the first time! They realize that perhaps they were reducing following Jesus to religious practice rather than daily relationship.

Practices are wonderful, but only if they help lead you to encounter God's voice and leadership.

GOD COMMUNICATES IN MYSTERIOUS WAYS

Earlier I mentioned that I have rarely heard of anyone who claimed to hear God's voice audibly or see God's handwriting on a wall as we read about in Scripture. However, of the countless conversations I have had on the subject of listening to and looking for God, I have heard a wide variety of ways God speaks to different people. It makes perfect sense that a God who has created a very diverse set of humans would relate differently to those communities and individuals.

There is no single formula for listening and responding to God, which makes sense when you think about how complex we are as human beings—not to mention the complexity of the God of the universe whom we are attempting to listen to. This complexity need not drive us away from our quest to discern what God is saying; rather, it could draw us deeper. We each get to decide which approach we will take, but I want to encourage you to be drawn into the deep waters of a life listening and responding to God.

Mike Breen has written a lot about following Jesus in our everyday lives and decisions. From him, I learned a phrase that has guided me in cutting through the complexity and discerning how God may be trying to get my attention. He calls these experiences where God is breaking into our lives "kairos moments."[10] The word *kairos* is one of the Greek words for time in the New Testament. Another word for time in Greek is *chronos*, from which we derive our English word "chronological." When we imagine time, we typically think of it on a timeline where time keeps on moving and none of us have the power to stop that reality.

Kairos time is different and tough to define because we don't have a word in English with the same meaning. Here is how I have come to understand it: kairos is the fullness of time, or a critical or opportune moment. When applied to the context in which Jesus uses the word, it is best understood as an inbreaking of God's kingdom or the Spirit of God breaking into our chronological time. For instance, in Mark 1:15, Jesus says, "The time [kairos] has come, the kingdom of God has come near."

When God is breaking into my everyday life and trying to get my attention about something, I want to be aware of this "kairos moment" because it's a key to how Jesus is leading in my life. From the time I have spent talking with others about how God moves in their lives, it's clear that these "moments" may look or feel very different for different people.

Of the many discussions I've had on the subject of discerning God's voice or movement, I want to summarize some common themes. I hope this can spark some interest in your life as to ways God may have been or is currently trying to get your attention or help you sort out the junk mail and see what invitations are coming from God.

Among these many different ways that folks have shared that God communicates with them, you'll notice something they all have in common: they are mysterious—just like God. It's important to let that mystery into your heart, because without it, skepticism and cynicism act as a vacuum that sucks any aspect of curiosity out of the proverbial room. Read these real-life examples with as much of an open mind as you can muster:

- Some have described having a reoccurring theme come up in their life. For instance, they read something that seems to connect with what someone shared. Then, in a time of reflection, they start to put together that this concept is not a one-off experience but a pattern in multiple areas of their life. Many say that this theme or thought lingers almost like it is following them, or it "stays with them" in their mind.

- Many describe encounters with the Bible or certain stories or concepts from Scripture that seem to come alive in a way that they hadn't before. I've heard people say that a part of a passage seemed to "jump off the page." It's almost as if God is using a cosmic highlighter to draw out a word or phrase. I have experienced a deep resonance with a character in Scripture that seems to be different from other times I've read the story. For example, as I read about Peter taking a step toward Jesus on the water, for an instant I feel as though my body and my hand are reaching out as I sink, and Jesus rescues me from the waves.

- Some people describe dreams, pictures, or visions that give them a window into something God may be saying. This happens to me frequently. I may be praying for someone and have no idea what to pray, and then God shows me a picture of something. It's usually very simple, like a child's playset or a forest with a small opening into a field. When I share it with others, they sometimes find it strange. Other times, they tear up because God is saying something to them through that picture that I don't understand at all. I've become comfortable with any reaction, knowing that sometimes it is from my own imagination and sometimes it is from God. I never suggest that I am certain something is from God, because remember, there is no such thing as certainty!

- People often share about times when they hear a word or phrase that comes out of nowhere or seems to be a novel thought—not something they have thought about before. They wonder if that could be God rather than their own will. Some describe being more certain when the phrase is not what they really *wanted* to hear. Often what they hear isn't audible but gives the same sensation as if something was whispered in their ear. Sometimes folks describe a sort of depth of knowing, as though they feel they know something deep in their soul even if there is not a lot of tangible evidence.

- Emotions are another way God speaks. A person may experience a strong emotion that seems to come from left field. Or they have a sense about something, and until they stop and pray, they can't "shake it off." People describe having a deep peace or even a deep angst. They realize that God is moving through their emotions, and there is something to discern from those feelings. One way I describe my discernment is a feeling of resonance or dissonance. There are times when I am asking God for guidance and I feel as if someone were playing beautiful harmonies on a piano—or alternatively, as though someone were slamming multiple keys and causing a horrible, dissonant sound to rise into the air.

- I have multiple friends and community members who describe a physical sensation they have when God is moving. Some describe an increased heart rate or a sense of their palms getting hot or burning when they know they are supposed to pray for someone or take a step of faith. Some feel a sense of physical heaviness over their body or even specific parts of their body. These sensations cause them to pay attention to something, and God leads them through this mysterious experience.

- Almost everyone I've talked to emphasized the importance of finding a trusted community to be a confirmation counsel and help you discern if what you are experiencing is from God. Even the wisest group cannot unlock God's mystery and know for certain what God may be saying or doing. But a trusted group of counselors—or a "clearness committee" as the Quaker tradition came to call it—can assure whether you should keep taking steps in the direction you are going or if you need to find a different route through discernment. While no other person can discern for you, often God does speak through another person as part of the process. More on the role of community in the next chapter.

- Finally, people often experience God's leadership in very tangible ways. A door seems to close or an opportunity becomes wide open, and it seems like God's hand was all over it. There are times when guidance from God seems to come in the form of a very tangible sign. Using the analogy from the previous chapter, I did once actually receive mail that was the final factor that led me to make one of the most important decisions in my life. I'll save that story for later.

Hopefully it's clear through all of these examples what I mean when I say that God communicates in mysterious ways. Being open to this mystery takes time and trust. The mystery of God's voice in our lives is much less like an army sergeant barking orders or a charismatic leader giving a strategic speech. Rather, it's more like the way that water "speaks" to the roots of plants. Here's what I mean: recent studies out of Australia show how, when seeking the needed water for growth, the roots of plants seem to listen for the sound of water and move toward the source, following the vibrations of the water. They listen for what sounds like the water source and then try to follow.[11] Jesus says he is the living water: "The one who believes in me (trusts me) will never be thirsty."[12] We are invited to listen for what sounds like the source of the living water and move in that direction.

5

LISTENING TO GOD TOGETHER

Who will listen and discern with me?

Who can be a part of my community of discernment?

We sat on the floor in their small living room so we wouldn't be too close to the nursery their baby was sleeping in. It was five of us women and my friend's husband. She had come to a crossroads in her vocation and didn't know what her next move should be. She had discussed with some of us individually the stress she was facing at work and her confusion about how she should be investing her time. She reached out and asked us to come together to help her discern the next step. We came with open hearts and minds and a ton of questions:

What gives you the most life right now?
What do you hear when you pray and listen to God?
What is the dynamic between you and your supervisor?
What transition has your team been going through?
Finally, we asked her husband, "What are you discerning
    when you pray for your wife?"

We were her clearness committee.

A dangerous temptation many of us have when it comes to discernment and decision-making is to make decisions alone, or with only our partner, or perhaps with a single friend. While that may be suitable for some of the everyday decisions of life, decisions that may significantly alter life's trajectory are best made with a clearness committee.

To use our scientific experiment analogy, consider that every well-done experiment relies on a team of experts. Usually, multiple people are working on the experiment itself, but long before any experimentation takes place, the team must dig into the existing research—past studies, experiments, and articles. You've probably also noticed that for any article to be taken seriously in the professional world, it must be "peer reviewed." Likewise, any good experiment relies on the work of many individuals. The same is true for us in the experiments of life.

Many groups within our faith tradition have held up the value of community discernment and listening to God together. The Catholic Jesuit tradition calls this practice "communal discernment," modeled after church father Ignatius of Loyola. Others in the contemplative tradition have "spiritual direction groups" that meet regularly. In the 1600s, the Quakers developed what were later termed *clearness committees*, acknowledging just how murky it can be to discern how God is leading us and showing us why we need others to help bring clarity. Others can help us listen to God but also access the wisdom God can give to each one of us if we ask for it.[1]

BARRIERS TO FINDING YOUR PEOPLE

Before we talk about how a clearness committee can function, let's be honest about something: many people don't have a community whom they would trust to discern with them. Don't get me wrong; most people have some good friends. But some friends are better at giving advice or have a hard time separating their experience and assumptions from the decision at hand.

Your clearness committee can include friends, but you shouldn't assume that all of your friends have the same ability to bring clarity and aid in discernment. Modern life doesn't lend itself well to having a group of people available to sit on your living room floor and process your vocation. What we did with my friend last year was not typical. It took many years to cultivate the kind of community that could gather and listen and ask questions as we did.

Dominant North American culture has a number of barriers to the development of the type of community with which we could form a clearness committee. One barrier is the glorification of marriage and the nuclear family. We have built up a caricature of the spouse as providing all someone needs in their life for support. This person should be able to meet your emotional, relational, and social needs. When they aren't able to, you have a best friend or confidant who can handle the rest. Reality check: your spouse and one other person are not a community. They can't take on the complexity of your life decisions as well as their own in the vacuum that a nuclear family so often becomes. And of course, many people don't have a spouse and don't plan to be married.

As a pastor, I am often approached by those who see my role as one of authority and hope that I can provide the answers they're looking for. You might view a psychologist, counselor, or mentor figure in your life similarly. While it can be great to get some feedback from these sorts of respected professionals, you need to be honest with yourself and be sure you truly want their nuanced feedback and are not hoping that they will simply tell you what to do. While I try to be someone who listens and helps ask good questions, many of us in helping professions are tempted to give in to that pull to just give answers to the person on the other end of the conversation. On my best days as a pastor, I encourage folks to find their clearness committee and not just rely on my thoughts or those of just one other important person in their life.

We are designed for community, not merely a couple of intense relationships. Community doesn't need to be a large group, but I hope you can build a community large enough that, at a given time, you can gather three or four others to help listen to God with you for significant life decisions.

Some of us may have had an intense experience of community in high school or college. This is not the case for everyone, but in the last thirty or forty years, the amount of people who have had a college or university experience that involved living with or near a community of friends has skyrocketed. While this can be a great experience in life for those privileged enough to have had this educational opportunity, it also creates some unrealistic expectations for future relationships.

Our experiences in college, or even high school, are unlike those we will have in any other aspect or period of our lives. We are all around the same age, all with the same goal, living in close proximity and seeing each other on a near-daily basis. Groups in those environments tend to form homogeneously—those of similar ethnic backgrounds and socioeconomic statuses tend to find each other to form their circle of friends.

While there are exceptions, a significant portion of the population is heading into their careers, or into life with small children, and then into middle age feeling as though nothing will ever be like that crew they had in high school, where everyone had known each other since first grade. Or nothing will be like that community formed in college, where you stayed up late having fun one night and the next stayed up talking about the meaning of life, God, and humanity. It will never be like that gap-year experience with that small group who traveled and served those in need around the world—everyone got so close!

Those experiences, if you were fortunate enough to have one, can be wonderful. They are like a pressure cooker for relationships, providing a rich experience in so much less time than it would take in any other circumstance. But no matter where you are in your life currently, no matter how far in the past that experience may be (if you had one at all), it's never too late to pursue true community in your life now. By pursuing community, you will find those among the group who can discern with you when it comes to your life-altering decisions.

DEVELOPING YOUR DISCERNMENT COMMUNITY

While everyone's situation is different, I have learned a few things over the years about what it looks like to find community in your life beyond those pressure-cooker experiences. First you need to make a commitment to yourself that you are going to persevere to develop community—this can't happen in a microwave "instant gratification" sort of way. Instead of a pressure cooker or microwave, the new relationships you're forming will be more like a Crock-Pot—they simmer slowly but deeply, which is how you find the rich community you are after.

Another hard reality we need to face is that developing community is not something you can outsource. You can't expect someone else to do this for you. While this may seem obvious, I often see people behave as though it's anyone else's fault but their own that they can't seem to find people whom they can trust and discern with. My church doesn't do small groups well enough, my supervisor doesn't create a team-building environment to build deep relationships, my spouse is more introverted/extroverted than me, and that complicates things. While any of these factors may be true, when I speak to those who are experiencing the depth of community I'm describing here, they didn't typically find it because their church or community center randomly assigned them to the same group. It isn't usually because the ice breakers were that good at the company BBQ, and it wasn't because they fit perfectly into the friend group their spouse already had when they met.

Typically, true community is found by those who commit to persevere, who stay open to new relationships, who make the first move in friendship, and who keep being intentional until relationships form the depth of trust needed for community. It can be awkward to be the one to ask for that other mom's contact info. It can feel strained to invite a single person over to dinner when you know your kids may throw food on the floor. It's stressful to try to deepen a causal friendship when you know you have very different backgrounds. But this is the work needed long before you're ready to begin praying and discerning about who might join your circle of trust when an important decision needs to be made in your life.

Let's get practical about how you could form your clearness committee when the time presents itself. You might have a group that remains consistent through a few of life's decisions. But perhaps more commonly, when you are approaching a certain decision in your life, you may select certain people who you feel are best suited to discern this specific question. I have used the words *group* and *committee*, and while this could be a group of people who live nearby and meet in person, it could also be a group of people from all over the country or world that meets online. In the example I gave at the beginning of the chapter, only four of us were there in person, and one was on an iPad on FaceTime.

While there is power in meeting together as a whole group for discernment, at times it may be more realistic to reach out to a handful of people individually and ask them to be a part of your discernment even if they never connect as a larger group. The most important thing is that others you trust are speaking into the decision. Remember, these folks are not going to tell you what to do. Nor do you need to accept all of their advice or thoughts. But the powerful act of the group listening together will offer a wisdom you cannot access on your own.

CLEARNESS COMMITTEE PROCESS

Parker Palmer is a spiritual writer and activist who has written about the clearness committee concept from the Quaker tradition.[2] Based on his writings, I have developed a simple outline to guide a clearness committee:

- The group commits to keep all that is shared confidential. If someone in the committee wants to take notes, they commit to guard those notes or dispose of them without betraying the trust of the group. The group should also agree on the time frame they will allot to this process so that everyone knows what to expect. The goal is not to solve this person's dilemma or make their decision for them, so the time frame will help determine the ending, when there may still be ambiguity.

- The person who is making the decision (sometimes more than one person is involved in the decision, like a couple or business partners, for example) shares a brief overview of the questions they are asking. These may be clear or still murky, but this is an important part of the process to try to articulate what is being discerned. They can then share any other important and relevant background information and any thoughts or hunches they have about what might be on the horizon. Sometimes it's helpful to limit the description to ten to fifteen minutes to allow sufficient time for the rest of the process.

- After the opening description, the group then responds with only clarifying or honest, open-ended questions. *Open-ended* means the questions should not be yes or no questions, but they should also not be "leading questions," where you are already assuming the answer.

- Normally, the focus person will answer the questions as they come, which will lead the group to deeper and deeper questions. However, the focus person has the right to choose not to answer any question. This doesn't mean the question isn't important or is answerable, but the person may take the question with them to process at a later time.

- The committee members must remember they are here to serve the focus person, not to interrogate them or pressure them. Be cognizant of the tone and pace of the conversation. It is normal for the focus person to feel very emotional. The committee should remain calm, compassionate, and careful in how they communicate. Here is how Palmer describes this critical factor in the process:

From the beginning to the end of the Clearness Committee, everyone must remain attentive to the focus person and his or her needs. This means suspending the normal rules of social gathering—no chitchat, no responding to other people's questions or to the focus person's answers, no joking to break the tension, no noisy and nervous laughter. We are simply to surround the focus person with quiet, loving space, resisting even the temptation to comfort or reassure or encourage this person, but simply being present with our attention and our questions and our care. If a committee member damages this ambiance with advice, leading questions, or rapid-fire inquisition, other members, including the focus person, have the right to remind the offender of the rules—and the offender is not at liberty to mount a defense or argue the point. The Clearness Committee is for the sake of the focus person, and the rest of us need to get our egos to recede.[3]

- When about fifteen minutes are left, someone in the committee should ask the focus person if they are willing to suspend the "questions only" rule and allow the committee members to reflect on what they have heard or state some observations they have made from listening. If the focus person says no, the questions should continue. Otherwise, each person should share concisely what they notice as well as mirror back what they have heard the person say.

- In the final five minutes, each committee member should share with the focus person some affirmations and encouragement that speaks more to their character than to the situation at hand. The focus person has been courageous and vulnerable, and this part of the process is important for their sense of emotional safety. The group can also reaffirm their commitment to confidentiality.

There are other formats for a process like this, but the most important thing is to invite others to be involved in the important decisions in life and invite them in with intention.

For examples of questions that can be asked during a clearness committee, check out the Decision-Making Toolbox in the appendix.

6

DECISION-MAKING ROAD BLOCKS

What could be holding me back from making a move?

*What may need to be addressed before I can
truly discern how God is leading me?*

I'm not sure how long I stood staring at the river after I hung up the phone. I must have been in some form of shock. Now that the decision was made, the panic attack of indecision seemed almost a distant memory. I had been walking through a local park by the Mississippi River near my house while talking on the phone. It was done—we had just ended our nearly three-year relationship right there on an iPhone. It stinks to break up over the phone, but since this was a long-distance relationship, it made no sense to fly the five hundred miles from Minnesota to Florida just to end the relationship. This final conversation was the ending of a long season of discernment trying to figure out what we were going to do, and it had finally come to a conclusion.

I'd love to say that in this moment I had a deep sense of peace that this was the *right* thing to do, but the reality is, I had no idea if this was the *right* thing. What I did feel on a deep level was that failing to make a move at this time would put me in a dangerous position.

You see, it was scary to think about ending something so meaningful. If I'm honest, I had a lot of fear in my heart and mind. I was afraid I had lost time that I could never get back, as a woman in my midthirties now, and was wondering if I should even stay on this dating bandwagon. I was afraid that he wasn't going to be OK as he continued to live into his sobriety. I was anxious about what this meant for the relationships we had formed as a couple and from each other's circles. The list could go on. But the fear I felt about whether the decision itself was right was the biggest barrier I faced in making the decision.

Like many people, I have a complicated relationship with the idea of right and wrong. There are general moral quandaries that everyone faces. We can get into debates about what is ethical in the many situations we face as humans. For example, we often debate what is right or wrong politically or the most ethical way to care for the environment or those in need. The more personal these moral or ethical questions become, the more stress they induce in our lives. All of these questions can really tie our minds up in knots.

As a child and young person, the idea of "the will of God" terrified me: What if I fall out of this will God has for me? Now that I have come to understand that God created me to make decisions in partnership with God's Spirit rather than as a pawn in God's proverbial chess game, this fear has not been as powerful.

However, I don't think the fear will ever leave me completely, because I do want to follow how God may lead! But for so many questions in life, I've come to see that following God's *way* has to overrule the idea of following God's *will*. It's become clear that out of his love for me, God invites me to make the next *best* decision in many circumstances rather than the only *right* decision.

Perhaps this tension is one we will always face if we truly want to follow God's Spirit. But our desire to get it right can paralyze us rather than truly be a way to honor God's leadership in our lives.

So even when we're feeling this tension and fear, we have to make what I call a "scary decision," because if we continue to stall and fail to make a move, it could become dangerous.

SCARY VERSUS DANGEROUS

There is a difference between scary and dangerous.

I've written before about Jim Koch, the cofounder of Boston Beer Company (producers of Samuel Adams beer), who says, "There are things in life that are scary, but not dangerous, but we're scared of them. And then there are things that are dangerous, but not scary. And those are the real problem. Those are the issue."[1] Koch came to a crossroads in his life where he knew that if he moved forward, it would be *scary* because he would be stepping deeper into uncertainty. But if he held back, it would be *dangerous* because it would be the beginning of the end of a dream. If he hadn't moved forward even though he was scared, he never would have built such a successful company.

At the end of that phone call, I was scared because I had no idea if I was making the right decision by ending that relationship. But if I hadn't made a move in one direction or the other, it would have been dangerous. It would have put me in danger of losing some of my own sense of self. I would have been in danger of missing out on what God may have had in store for me, either beyond this relationship *or* if I would have decided to go all-in on the relationship. Being stuck in paralyzing indecision wasn't getting me anywhere, and in time, I believe it would have damaged my heart and soul.

If you are like me and you have a complicated relationship with doing what is right, then know you aren't alone. I have had this conversation with so many people. We can see in the stories in the Bible that we aren't alone when it comes to history either! Many if not most characters in Scripture who were trying to follow God's leadership in their lives were wrestling with the question, What is the right thing to do?

How about Joseph, the earthly father of Jesus? He was shocked to find out his fiancée was pregnant. He was going to divorce her quietly because he was a "righteous man." He had to divorce Mary by law because that was the "right" thing to do at the time. Because he was a kind man or a good man, he was going to do that quietly. So when he decided to stay with Mary, it was a big deal.

He had to push past what was scary to end up stepping into the bigger story God was telling. It was a pretty important role he had to play! Joseph's adoption of Jesus, which took place culturally the moment he named Jesus after he was born, was the way Jesus was included in the royal line of David. It was critical to show that Jesus was fulfilling the prophecy found in places like Isaiah. Angel or no angel, I'm sure Joseph wasn't completely certain he was doing the right thing when he decided to stay with Mary. But he made a move, and it made all the difference in the end.

HOW SURE IS SURE?

How sure do we need to be in order to take steps into the future when we aren't certain what we should do? It should be no surprise for me to remind you that there is no way to be 100 percent certain. Remember, we can have assurance but not certainty.

How sure, or full of assurance, do you need to be before you make a move? If you can't have 100 percent assurance, are you someone who shoots for 80 percent? Or are you able to take the next step at just 55 or 60 percent? This will depend on a combination of your risk tolerance and your level of experience with the type of decision at hand. There is nothing wrong with being someone with a low or high risk tolerance. What is important is that you recognize that about yourself. You may discover that you are someone who jumps the gun, starting your sprint before it's time. Or maybe you are someone who stays at the starting block way too long, sometimes taking yourself out of the race completely.

Take some time to define your risk tolerance. To guide you, I have a risk-tolerance assessment in the appendix. Then you can consider if some risk management can be helpful when it comes to your decision. This may mean getting others involved, doing some extra math, or calculating how things may affect others in your sphere. There is one way to most effectively manage risk, and that is to move forward one experiment at a time, breaking a big decision down into lower-risk actions you can take.

It's also important to note that we are living in a time when we have developed what I call "a culture of indecision." There have never been more options in front of us for many of the decisions we have to make, from the grocery store, to online shopping, to the growing diversity of the job market, to the online dating scene. The increase in modes of communication has not always strengthened communication; rather, it sometimes has given way to even more wavering when it comes to decisions. Take, for instance, how people make plans to connect socially. We often use text messaging to wait until the last minute to decide if we will participate rather than making a commitment to connect with friends and holding to those plans. But the culture of indecision does not have to hold us back.

In the next section of the book, we will focus on various experiments that can help you make decisions in different areas of life. In the appendix, I also offer some of my best decision-making tools that I've discovered or designed over the years. There is no perfect formula that will lead you to the right decision, but I promise you will be well on your way to discerning through movement one experiment at a time if you break down the experiments into steps that help you manage your risk tolerance.

OTHER BARRIERS TO CONSIDER

In addition to the barriers of always wanting to get it right and having a low risk tolerance, I want you to consider a few other things that could be barriers for you. If you don't address these factors first, you could move to part 2 of this book, where we get very nitty-gritty and practical, and be very disappointed. You'll find out it's no use going through the experiments if any of these realities are holding you back.

First I want to remind you of the focus of the previous chapter. Without involving others in your experiments, you can hit dead ends that could have otherwise been avoided with the counsel and wisdom of others.

Another barrier can be your emotions. Your emotions certainly play an important role in your decision-making. It is critical to take into account how you feel. Remember how often in the examples of hearing from God people mentioned how they felt? The problem is, our emotions can sometimes hijack our minds and get us stuck. Certain emotions tend to do this more than others. My observation has been that fear, bitterness, and fatigue are at the top of the list of what can hold us back from making the moves we need to make in life. Perhaps you'd add something else to the list in your own life. It's a great step to be able to name what your sabotaging emotion may be.

Fear of getting it wrong is an example of how fear can hold us back, but fear can show up in sneaky ways! Perhaps you are discerning God's leadership to deepen your relationships with people who are different from you—fear of difference can keep us from amazing relationships we could otherwise have. Fear shows up when we want certainty so badly that we end up terrified of the unknown. We can then catastrophize and freak ourselves out about what *could* be up ahead even though those things are very unlikely. Finally, fear can become paralyzing when it's connected to trauma in our lives. Experiences that have stuck with us in negative ways can significantly hold us back. I highly suggest processing these experiences with a counselor or therapist. This has been critical for me to be able to work through my own trauma.

Bitterness is another emotion that can take us down easily. If our trust was betrayed or people didn't live up to our expectations, we can become bitter. This can also happen in our relationship with God. We may be holding on to bitterness from our last big decision if we feel like God failed to lead or protect us. When it comes to paralyzing bitterness, we need to address the root of it. Was it a relationship, a faith community, or an experience with God or a friend? Where did the trust begin to decay? Not identifying the root is like only tearing off the leaves of a weed—it's going to grow back!

I have been an activist most of my adult life—I am committed to taking action on the things God puts on my heart. I march against racial injustice and actively pursue inner change in my life and my community. I constantly ask how I can take action for the poor, which has led me to travel around the world, as well as next door, to give time, energy, and financial support. I try to show my neighbors the love Jesus told us to have for the world, which has resulted in some very long, awkward conversations in my yard with neighbors over the years. However, they probably think of *me* as the awkward neighbor!

Taking action is important to me, but it can lead to physical, emotional, and spiritual fatigue. You may have other realities that have led to fatigue, but what is true for us all is that when we are tired, it's very hard to discern and stay alert to see what God is doing around us. I've heard people say those who are extremely tired are just as dangerous behind the wheel of a car as someone driving drunk. This is true for being behind the wheel of our lives as well. We aren't going to stay on the road if we fall asleep at the discernment wheel. This is why holistic well-being is so critical in our lives.

If we can overcome these barriers in life, we will be ready to step into the story God has invited us to join. God cares about our decisions because our stories are a part of God's greater story. The next chapter offers some initial questions we can ask regarding the gray areas of life and gives us a framework for how our stories are a part of God's story. Then we'll be all set to design our experiments and make a move.

Check out the Well-Being Wheel in the Decision-Making Toolbox in the appendix to discover how you can grow in your well-being in order to gain the energy and strength needed to listen and respond to God.

7

FAITHFUL IMPROVISATION

What do I do when the decision is in a gray area of life?

What does my discernment have to do with God's story?

Adulthood has this way of giving you hindsight bias. You look back on your experiences and realize that in the past, you may have overlooked or underappreciated what you had, such as when you think about childhood and your relationship with your parents or other adults. My dad passed away when I was seventeen, so when I look back over twenty years ago since my last conversation with him, I find it harder and harder to remember those conversations with clarity.

As an adult, I see how the adolescent version of me thought my dad must have had everything figured out—like most adults, right? As we each become adults and notice the ways we are still learning and growing, we realize that the adults who came before us didn't have it figured out either. It can be a rude awakening. In hindsight, I can see how my dad was just trying to figure out life, faith, and everything else. I look back on one set of memories with my dad and realize that I actually *under*appreciated what he was trying to share with me. It was a short set of questions he called "the gray test."

The gray test was one of the decision-making tools he shared with me when I was a teenager. I was firmly in the eye-roll stage of life, and I couldn't see how helpful it was until I had to make the weighty decisions that come with adulthood. So as my father's daughter, I want to offer the next generation a version of this test. I've found this test is an important tool to be used before crafting an experiment regarding a decision. It can help clarify what your actual questions are in the disorienting areas of life.

Many decisions in life are "gray" or seem as though they aren't black or white. For these situations, we can use the gray test— some questions that can help us find clarity in the gray scenarios of life:

1. Am I letting this decision be influenced by my understanding of Scripture and God's best for God's children?
2. Is this choice going to help me grow spiritually, or could it deter my spiritual growth and maturity?
3. How might this decision enhance or harm my ability to be a witness of the love of Jesus to my neighbor?
4. Would this choice encourage and uplift others in my community or family? Or would it discourage or harm the greater body of Christ?
5. Imagine Jesus with you in person. How might he respond to your options when it comes to this decision? What would it feel like to take a step with Jesus right there with you?
6. How does this decision fit within the greater story of God, which guides our stories?

This "test" is not a formula—as I mentioned before, we all hear from God in different ways—but I have found that it can help me get a bit of clarity when I find myself overwhelmed by confusion. Every once in a while, one of these questions helps me realize that a decision I am facing is not as *gray* as I thought it was. Truly imagining Jesus with me or thinking about how this decision affects my community or my neighbors can at times snap me into a reality check that a decision is clearer than it had appeared.

So take a minute and apply the gray test to a decision in your life. For many decisions, after asking these questions, you will still face uncertainty about what to do. That's OK! It's just good to start with these questions to expand your current thinking about the situation and ensure that there isn't an answer that could save you the time and energy needed for the deep work of discernment on the gray areas of life.

The rest of this book will discuss just how we can approach these gray decisions, of which we face many in our lives. But where do we go after the gray test? If you get to the sixth question of the gray test and are still wavering, then a deep dive into question six is a great next step: How does this decision fit within the greater story of God, which guides our stories? To dig in, may I suggest a little improv?

TINA FEY AND THE RULES OF IMPROV

In Tina Fey's book *Bossypants*, she discusses the four rules of improv comedy:

1. "The first rule of improvisation is AGREE. Always agree and SAY YES."
2. "The second rule of improvisation is not only to say yes, but YES, AND."

3. "The next rule is to MAKE STATEMENTS. . . . 'Don't ask questions all the time.'"
4. "THERE ARE NO MISTAKES, only opportunities."[1]

I know that life is not the same as improv comedy, but go with me on this! These rules really can be helpful when it comes to trying to understand our story within God's greater story. Let's apply these four rules to our responses as characters in the story God is writing and invites us to join.

Rule 1—agree and say yes to God. Who does God say you are? What is your identity as a child of God and a follower of Jesus? Say yes and agree with God in your life, and you'll find yourself becoming more and more fully who God made you to be!

But don't stop there; move to rule number 2. Agree, but then say "and," then tangibly step into that reality. For instance, you might say, "I agree with you, God, that you created me as a person passionate about justice for those on the margins. *And* I am going to start experimenting with ways to live out this passion in tangible ways."

Then there is rule number 3—make statements and don't just ask questions all the time. It's true that when we are trying to make decisions, we often have a lot of questions. But could we also discover statements we could make? For instance, a question could be "Should I take my passion for justice toward a change in my paid career or vocation?" Instead of getting stuck in that question, you could make a statement like "I know that there are volunteer opportunities with the refugee resettlement agency my church partners with. I will reach out and see what I can fit in my schedule alongside my work." This could get you closer to an experiment in this area that could help you discern God's future for you. It all starts with saying, "Yes, and . . ."

The final rule is that there are no mistakes. But here's the thing: we are humans in real lives, not comedy shows (even when life feels like a comedy . . . or a tragicomedy). So we do make mistakes sometimes. But even when we look back and wish we would have made a different decision, we do have opportunities—opportunities to learn from our mistakes, make things right when our mistakes have affected others, and receive forgiveness from God, who is full of love and mercy. The mistakes from our past that haunt us—or the fear, and the reality, that we will make mistakes in the future—are all opportunities if we choose to see them that way.

A BONUS RULE OF IMPROV

No offense to Tina or any other improv comedians who may be reading this, but there is something in God's story that no other improv sketch offers: We know how the story ends. We have glimpses throughout the Bible of the future God has for us. The last book of the Bible, Revelation, is written in what is called apocalyptic literary form, with lots of images and pictures that represent deep concepts. But even with its mystery, it paints a picture of the end of the story where all the wrong things are made right and there is no more crying, pain, or suffering. It's God's unveiling of the deepest "happily ever after" you could ever find. In some ways, every other story that ends with a "happily ever after" reflects the yearning of the human soul for God's future permanent happily ever after.

Knowing the end of the story means we get to add a final rule of improv to life following Jesus:

5. Stay faithful to the end of the story.

Theologian N. T. Wright writes about what he calls faithful improvisation:[2] that God's story is like a play with five acts. They are all pointing to God's grand conclusion: creation, fall, Israel, Jesus, and the church.[3]

We are living smack in the middle of act 5, and remember, we have a very intense and amazing picture of the end of the story. We know how act 5 is going to come to a grand ending. But as actors in this play, we are at this messy middle moment where, all of a sudden, there is no script—awkward! God is the main character, and we are supporting characters to the most important story ever told . . . but there is no script for this part of this important story!

What do we do now?

Well, the actors would improvise. But they would need to improvise *faithfully*.

Here is what Wright says on the subject: "We must act in the appropriate manner for this moment in the story; this will be in direct continuity with the previous acts (we are not free to jump suddenly to another narrative, a different play all together), but such continuity also implies discontinuity, a moment where genuinely new things can and do happen. We must be ferociously loyal to what has gone before and cheerfully open to what must come next . . . all actors are free to improvise their own fresh scenes . . . but no actor is free to improvise scenes from another play, or one with a different ending."[4]

To be faithful to the story, the actors let the history from the first four acts guide where the story will continue to go. They don't break character; they remember who they are and whose they are. They may continue the story in innovative and creative ways, but the story is always pointing toward and anticipating the conclusion.

It's tempting to think we are the main characters of the story and thus declare, "I will write my own story however I want, thank you very much!" But when we accept that we are characters in God's story, then we can't break character and forget we are children of God and followers of Jesus—even when some decisions would be easier if we *were* someone else. Even if we have a lot of creative license to make decisions within the story, if we surrender ourselves to God, then we are part of a story that is always pointing toward the conclusion. It comes back to truly wanting to hear God's voice rather than narrate our own story.

We've all been in situations where we know we have left God's narrative behind, thinking that choosing to change directions will somehow still get us where we want to go. But if we trust God's love for us, then even when we leave the narrative, our gut reaction to ourselves or others should be "Whoa, wait . . . where am I going? I know where God's story, and thus my story, ends. Why am I venturing off in a totally different direction?"

So let's take note when we see that a decision is taking us out of God's story, because it is actually motivated by greed or selfishness. Let's pay attention when we are drawn to make a choice that we know is not ultimately about loving our neighbor as ourselves. Check in with yourself, someone you trust, or your clearness committee when you wonder if your decisions are coming from a place of undervaluing yourself or others.

These are crossroad moments where we can choose to get back on the trajectory toward the grand finale of God's story. This is in part what the prophet Jeremiah meant when he shared God's words with God's people thousands of years ago: "Stand at the crossroads and look; ask for the ancient paths, ask where the good way is, and walk in it, and you will find rest for your souls."[5]

PART 2

I DARE YOU TO MOVE

We see in order to move;
we move in order to see.

—William Gibson

8

DESIGNING EXPERIMENTS

What is the question I am asking?

What are the next steps in designing an experiment?

"Indecision is still a decision." As soon as the words left my lips, I doubted that I should have uttered them in the first place. I sat with a friend who was stuck—paralyzed by indecision. I had been there before myself, and even more often I had sat across from someone with the same pained look on their face.

I searched his face for a reaction, since it felt like the statement was hanging in the air. I was ready for anything, from witnessing a grown man burst into tears to storming out of the room.

He took a deep breath and let out a sigh. I was relieved when he said, "Oh my, you are so right . . . I've got to make a decision."

That was the day he truly began the search for a new career. Sitting behind a desk for eight hours was neither suiting his personality nor serving his mental well-being. But when he thought about a career change, he only saw an endless sea of other options. The sheer volume of options had been holding him back from making a move and beginning to truly discover what other careers could be available to him. All I knew was that someone outgoing, creative, and innovative was literally trapped in a cubicle.

Indecision is still a decision. We can trick ourselves into believing that there is wisdom in waiting and holding out for "the right time" or for "something better to come up." Sometimes waiting is the right thing to do, but many times it is actually an excuse that holds us back from making a call we need to make. Author and psychologist Meg Jay puts it this way: "We think that by avoiding decisions now, we keep all of our options open for later—but not making choices is a choice all the same"[1] It was in her book *The Defining Decade* that I first heard about the jam experiment.[2]

In 2000, psychologists Sheena Iyengar and Mark Lepper created an experiment that compared a display of twenty-four gourmet jams at a market with a display of only six jams at that same market. While the large jam display with twenty-four different options proved to be more enticing—that is, more people came over to peruse the various types than the display with only six options—the major finding in this study was that only 3 percent of those who came to check out the twenty-four jams actually purchased one, and 30 percent of those who came over to the display with six jams purchased one. The table with more options received more attention but fewer buyers. This study has been reproduced with everything from beer to jeans. Time and time again, the results show decision paralysis when there are too many options.

Sometimes we find ourselves stuck because we feel like we don't have any options. Other times there are too many. In either case, the only way to get unstuck is to make a move.

STAY OUT OF THE DITCHES

Imagine you are driving on one of those dirt roads that has a ditch on both sides. As you work on getting unstuck and making a move, your goal is to stay on the road and out of either ditch. One ditch represents a sort of haphazard wandering—you make a move that is not very thoughtful or intentional just to get going. The idea is sometimes stated as "taking a stab at it" or "throwing things to the wall to see what sticks." Most of the time, this approach doesn't work out because so little discernment is involved in "just giving something a try." For low-risk decisions, like trying out a new hobby, that may work just fine. But when it comes to finding a new career, making a decision about purchasing a home, or moving to another city, this approach doesn't get us far, and we can easily end up stuck once again.

On the other side of the road is the ditch that represents the need to have a full-fledged strategic plan in order to make a move. It can be tempting to wait until we have a foolproof plan that includes three other backup plans before we make a decision. This is so enticing because it gives an illusion that uncertainty can be taken out of the equation. While plans and strategy can help mitigate some uncertainty, waiting for the perfect strategic plan can actually keep us from hearing what God may be saying along the way. We can become rigid and stuck to the plan because it gives us a false sense of security and control in the situation.

As we navigate through our lives, we may end up driving off into one of these ditches. Just like in a car, when we end up in one ditch, we can overcorrect and head right into the opposite ditch. This is a problem not just in our personal lives but also with decisions humans make regarding organizations, communities, or businesses.

In this part of the book, I'm going to walk you through some thoughtfully designed experiments that will help you stay on the road. But I'm not the only person to try to come up with a solution to this ditch problem. At the d.school at Stanford University, they teach a process called "design thinking."[3] Design thinking is a practical and intentional approach to problem-solving and decision-making that integrates empathy, creativity, and experimenting. This approach has proven to lead to innovation and better outcomes than traditional methods of decision-making or strategic planning. It also creates space for spiritual discernment in ways that traditional plans and techniques for problem-solving do not.

Here is how the Stanford d.school describes their purpose: "We believe everyone has the capacity to be creative. We build on methods from across the field of design to create learning experiences that help people unlock their creative potential and apply it to the world. Design can be applied to all kinds of problems. But, just like humans, problems are often messy and complex—and need to be tackled with some serious creative thinking."[4]

The core abilities they hope to see grow in those participating in the d.school—like navigating ambiguity, learning from others, synthesizing information, and experimenting rapidly—illustrate why this approach can be so helpful in our conversation on discernment and decision-making. If this process is helpful to those thinking through business decisions and problems facing humanity at large, then let's be sure to glean what can help us as we move forward in our process of designing thoughtful experiments for the decisions we face in our own lives. The d.school offers a number of free online resources if you want to dig even further. But let me pull out a few perspectives I have learned from the design thinking process that can help us design the experiments needed to make a move while staying on the road and out of the decision-making ditches.

LISTEN AND EMPATHIZE

The starting place for the design thinking process is listening and empathizing. When someone is trying to figure out the right product for a consumer, understanding their clientele is key. For our purposes, we've already learned how listening to God is crucial to this process. Also, hearing from mentors, friends, and your community—like the clearness committee described in part 1—is an important aspect of discernment.

Many of the personal decisions we make affect others in our lives, so empathizing with how they may feel about the present situation and possible ways forward is another important component of listening. Finally, we need to figure out how to listen to ourselves. How can we listen to our thoughts, our emotions, and even what our physical body may be trying to tell us? Each of these ways of listening should be included in this critical first step.

For me, journaling is a great way to list all of the listening I have done in the process of trying to move forward. You could even just keep a running list or a set of bullet points. This gives you a chance to look for themes or surprises and also helps you go deeper than what may seem obvious on the surface of a problem or decision. Listening, especially to ourselves and God, gives us clues for the next stage of design thinking.

DEFINE THE PROBLEM OR QUESTION

Those who engage in the process of design thinking start planning their experiments only after making sure that they are asking the best question. In design thinking, this is usually referred to as defining the actual problem. What is the actual question you are asking? This could seem obvious at first. For instance, you may be asking, "Should we have a third child?"

But when you engage in the listening process, you might discover that the actual question you are hoping to answer in your life is "What would bring the most purpose and meaning in this season?" Children can offer a deep sense of purpose for many, but a couple may realize they need to design a different set of experiments if the deeper question is about purpose and not only family size. Sometimes I call this "the question beneath the question."

Another example may be a question like "Should I apply for that open position at work that would be a promotion?" When you collect all of the listening results, you may realize the question is actually "Is there a different career path I may need to make altogether?" Applying for the next rung up the ladder seems like common sense in our world today, but it can actually lead to the ditch of just wandering and doing the next thing that comes along. Sometimes I call this "the question beneath the obvious question." It can feel daunting to recognize the deeper questions, but asking those deeper questions prevents us from wasting time designing experiments that don't get at the core of our questions. It can also lead us where we never dreamed we would be! Discernment from God can lead us from surviving to thriving.

IDEATE

Hasso Platner from Stanford describes this part of the process this way: "Ideate is the mode in which you generate radical design alternatives. Ideation is a process of 'going wide' in terms of concepts and outcomes—a mode of 'flaring' instead of 'focus.'

The goal of ideation is to explore a wide solution space—both a large quantity and broad diversity of ideas."[5] To some personality types, this can seem like a waste of time because many of the ideas in that "wide solution space" are not realistic or actionable. However, when you take the lid off of the ideation box and open yourself to "out of the box" ideas, you may find yourself led in a completely different direction than if you were to narrow your focus prematurely. God created us as creative people, and it would be a shame not to make space for creativity in our process.

A family of four that I know well had an unsettling feeling like they were being confined and held back from something. It started with the wife, then her husband, so they brought it up to their teenage children and found out that even they had a sense something just wasn't right. They weren't sure what it was. They loved their home, their neighborhood, and their friends. School was going well, and their jobs were going fine. So as a family, they decided to listen, figure out what questions they were asking, and be open to whatever ideas might arise. With a couple of teenagers, you can imagine that some ideas were far from reality! In the end, this family made a huge move across the country to join a community they felt called to in pursuit of their purpose. They ended up moving from Minnesota to Portland, Oregon, for a few months, then to Montana, and then (I kid you not) their final destination ended up being Portland, Maine. I asked if they thought they misheard God and went to the wrong Portland the first time, but they are pretty sure God had purpose for their time in both Portlands! They are still living into that life-changing adventure today!

For most of us, the ideation phase won't lead to a cross-country move, multiple Portlands, or something else that radical. However, to undertake the exercise of ideation, you may need to work through your fears of uncertainty and your risk-tolerance struggles. This is an important part of the process.

DESIGN AN EXPERIMENT AND GET STARTED

Stanford calls this "prototype and test," which sounds about right when you are launching an app or a possible solution to a higher-ed conundrum.[6] As discussed earlier, I love the term *experiment* because it reminds us of some critical factors.

We may have a hunch, but we don't know the results or answer quite yet. An experiment offers clear steps to keep us from being stuck. There is space in this experiment to wonder what God's Spirit may be doing or saying to us as we proceed. We can start to make a move and give something a try before we have a full-fledged strategic plan. Often an experiment gives us a chance to make lower-risk decisions before making a larger, more significant decision.

It's time to design your experiment! Let's bring back the steps outlined in the first chapter of this book:

Step 1: Define your question—or what you are hoping to learn.

Step 2: Do your research and creative brainstorming—see what has been learned and what answers have been discovered by others in the past. Also make sure you consider various creative options for the experiment itself.

Step 3: Determine the first experiment you will try that will answer your question or help you learn more.

Step 4: Name the steps of your experiment and execute them for a predetermined amount of time.

Step 5: Analyze and review the results and determine what was learned.

Listening is the prework for the experiment, but steps 1 and 2 should sound similar to the steps in the d.school process we've been discussing. So now we come to step 3, and it's time to choose an experiment to try. This can be a tough spot for many scientists. If you know what you want to learn, the best experiment may not always be obvious at first. The rest of the chapters of part 2 will help you determine a good experiment to start with. It is not unusual to end up needing to engage in a series of experiments. This is similar in scientific study—there are very few stand-alone experiments. Rather, the lessons from one experiment are applied to the next and so on.

Step 4 is very important—you have to define the steps of the experiment. The goal is to make the steps as clear and actionable as possible. When I lead others through designing experiments for life's decisions, oftentimes this is where they get stuck—they don't provide enough detail. You want to almost feel like you're going overboard on the level of detail and the clarity of these steps. The reality is, as humans, we take things one step at a time, and when we don't outline the steps, we can't complete the experiment. Months or years later, we'll look back and think, "Why didn't I try that experiment I designed?" And it all comes down to not breaking down the steps in enough detail and clarity. We will dig into this as we design experiments in the coming chapters.

An important value of d.school is that we don't merely learn by thinking; we also learn by doing. At some point, mere thinking will hold us back. Making a move is key to getting unstuck, learning what we are hoping to learn, and making the decisions that can lead us to the future God has in store for us.

Are you ready to start experimenting?

OK, let's run through a checklist to be sure that you are ready to start designing your experiments. This list outlines what we have covered from part 1 until now. If you aren't ready to check off something on this list, then perhaps it is best to look back a few chapters before moving forward:

- Are you spiritually prepared to release the idea that there is only one right "will" for your life and to entrust your life to God's "way" of leading you through the messiness of life's decisions?
- Do you trust that God wants to speak to you, and are you surrendered to Jesus's leadership in your life?
- Are you open to the various ways God may speak to you, recognizing that God's Spirit may move in new ways in this season of your life if you are looking for it?
- Do you know who is on your clearness committee, and have you created time to hear from them and listen to what God may say through them?
- Have you examined your life for possible roadblocks that could stop your experiment in its tracks or before it gets started?
- Have you submitted your decision to the "gray test" outlined in chapter 7?
- Are you ready to live by the rules of improv, since experiments often require improvisation?
- Have you collected everything you've heard through listening to God, others, and your own heart and mind?
- Have you left some space for ideating and using your God-given creativity so that you are truly open to however God may lead you?

If you can complete this checklist, then it's time to design your first experiment! The next few chapters break down the various types of experiments you may want to try. Once you define the question you are asking, you will know what type of experiment you need to design. However, many questions fall into a few categories. Don't let that hold you back! You may find that more than one of the following chapters helps you define the first experiment, so don't spend too much time trying to narrow down your decision to only one of the following types. Life is much more complex than the categories we often try to fit it into. Embrace the messiness while at the same time focusing your energy on only one or two experiments at a time.

I promise you that after you get started on an experiment, you will learn by doing and quickly discover a new perspective. This will help you get unstuck and put you well on your way to discernment through movement.

9

SPIRITUAL LIFE EXPERIMENTS

Experiments about experiencing God and a life of faith.

I laid on my back, staring at the ceiling at my physical therapist's office. I had thrown my back out yet again, and he was trying to help me stretch out the muscles that had gotten themselves all tied up in knots. All I wanted was to be able to move again without searing pain shooting through my spine.

"Why does this keep happening? How do I keep finding myself back here again flat on my back in pain?" I groaned, assuming he would understand that this was a rhetorical question meant to give me a way to lament my situation, not a question that he should actually answer. He didn't realize this, and instead, he launched into a very practical response: "As you go around in your everyday life, your body is making choices about how it responds to what you are asking it to do. So when you reach over to pick something up, or when you lift something heavy, your muscles start to respond and react to help you do that activity. The problem is, your body doesn't always choose the right muscles for the job. Your body will always choose the path of least resistance, but that path is not always what is best for your body."

He went on to explain how this "path of least resistance" strategy causes some of my core muscles to be weaker than they are supposed to be, and thus when a strain happens in my back, those muscles fail to do their job, causing inflammation in the muscles that my body has defaulted to make that movement happen. I was in too much pain at the time to realize this statement's deep relevance for life, but now that I am out of the woods with my back pain, I see how this is a perfect illustration for our lives of faith.

Most of the time, I go through my day without putting much thought into how I exist in the world. I tend to choose the path of least resistance when it comes to processing what is going on around me and the thoughts swirling around in my mind and heart. This seems like it's working well for me until there is an unusual strain in my life, and then it's as though I spiritually throw my back out and find myself staring at the ceiling of my life, wondering how I got back here again.

Maybe this experience resonates with you. I know that for many of us, the COVID-19 pandemic has provided a very clear example of just how much we had failed to spiritually "strengthen the core" so to speak. It has acutely reminded me how critical spiritual practices are for helping me stay strong in the face of weeks without leaving the house and feelings of isolation and fear of getting sick.

My physical therapist gave me some exercises to try to strengthen the muscles that had failed to do their job so that perhaps I wouldn't injure my back again. But then he said two things that were very important for my physical next steps, and now I can see they are just as important for our spiritual next steps.

First, he said that my body can't get stronger and heal while it is inflamed: "I know you are going to want to fix this problem and start the exercises to get strong again. But first you need to do the stretches I will show you, rest your back, and use ice regularly to decrease the swelling." That guy sure was reading my mind. I hated this pain, and I was ready for a quick fix back to strength, but first I needed to pay attention to where I was inflamed and bring that swelling down.

I'm not sure what spiritual question you may be asking, but before we take steps to design an experiment to move forward, it's important to stop and see if there is inflammation where some healing needs to take place. If so, then perhaps our first experiment is actually about how to pursue that healing and bring that inflammation down. Maybe you thought your question was "How can I reconnect with God?" but the question beneath the question is actually "How can I heal from the spiritual wounds from my parent/church/mentor?" or "How can I get emotional healing from the loss or trauma I've experienced?"

Healing is not a perfect formula, which is often why experiments are necessary. There's a reason doctors call it "practicing medicine." The way the body heals doesn't always follow a prescribed plan. But doctors and nurses have learned some great places to start. The same is true for our hearts spiritually and emotionally.

Many have found the next steps in healing through a counselor or therapist. Others have found that a practice of journaling and writing about what they have experienced is key. Another great experiment would be to try to work the twelve steps of Alcoholics Anonymous. Trust me, you don't need to have an addiction to seek freedom from what you have experienced. These steps have brought healing to many. I recommend the book *Journey to Freedom* by Scott Reall.[1] I know many people who have gone through this book on their own or with some friends, and it has led them to a place of healing that helped the swelling come down and gave them the freedom to step into new experiments in their spiritual lives.

Perhaps one of these ideas will help you determine your first experiment if you need to heal your mind and heart. It really is OK to think of calling a counselor as an experiment. Perhaps you have been skeptical in the past, and that's fine. Give it a try and see what you can learn from the experience that can help you move forward.

EXERCISES ARE NOT ENOUGH

The second thing my physical therapist said was that just doing the stretches and exercises was not enough: "You need to increase your awareness of how you are or aren't using your muscles all the time, in everything that you do. Without intention, your body will continue to choose the path of least resistance, and you will inevitably overuse some muscles and misuse and underuse others."

Spiritual practices are important, but there is also a reason we call them *practices*: working on the "spiritual muscles" in our hearts and minds will give us muscle memory that we can draw on in our everyday lives. The experiments we can design to take the next steps in our spiritual lives can help us get unstuck or move forward. But we have to be intentional so that what we learn in these experiments can become part of our way of life. Without this intentionality, we will find ourselves right back where we started.

In my book *Stay Curious: How Questions and Doubts Can Save Your Faith*, I tackle the question of spiritual experiments head-on for the entire book. I will share here some of the key aspects of designing spiritual experiments, but I recognize that your spirituality is critical to all aspects of your life. So if this area requires a series of deep experiments, I highly recommend you check out *Stay Curious* and the many experiment ideas I share in that resource.

A few questions and themes seem to come up over and over again when I come alongside others who are struggling to make decisions and move forward in their spiritual lives. I've noticed the following themes: relating and reconnecting to God, rebuilding trust with God, relating to a faith community (or lack thereof), learning how to engage with God or others when you have experienced some shifts in your understanding of faith, and experiencing questions and even doubts about God, faith, the Bible, or the church.

SPACE FOR LAMENT

Every once in a while, someone designs a faith experiment rooted in an exciting journey or prompting from God. But most of the time, these themes come with some intense and often painful emotions. The most encouraging thing I can share with you is how normal these feelings are. The Bible gives us an invitation for what to do with these emotions and feelings, and we call this process *lament*—a practice of crying out to God in anguish, frustration, pain, or grief. We may even have some anger we need to express to God. We see lament throughout Scripture, but especially in the Psalms—in fact, in Psalms alone, more psalms or songs are laments to God than offerings of thanks!

One I often turn to is Psalm 27. Listen to verses 8 and 9:

Hear my voice when I call, Lord;
be merciful to me and answer me.
My heart says of you, "Seek his face!"
Your face, Lord, I will seek.
Do not hide your face from me,
do not turn your servant away in anger;
you have been my helper.
Do not reject me or forsake me,
God my Savior.[2]

In Psalm 42, we hear the Psalmist say repeatedly, "Why, my soul, are you downcast? Why so disturbed within me?"[3]

If these statements are seen as acceptable in Scripture, then they should be acceptable for us, as we are vulnerable with God and others we trust. Unfortunately, not everyone will react with understanding when you choose to share what may be on your heart. The most important thing to know is that God is not anxious about our anxiety, even if other people are. Jesus can handle our questions—all of them—even if some people seem unable to hold the tension.

STEPS TO DESIGNING SPIRITUAL LIFE EXPERIMENTS

Remember, the first step is to listen and learn. This may mean talking with others in your life whom you respect or whose thoughts you trust. Perhaps you might choose to read some books or listen to some podcasts. A quick warning as you listen to the perspectives of others: sometimes our faith questions cause so much tension that we can easily latch on to the thoughts and theories of the first spiritual guru whose words connect with us.

Proverbs suggests that there is wisdom in a multitude of counselors.[4] We may be tempted to want someone else to do the intellectual and spiritual heavy lifting for us. But you have to do your own work of integrating your faith in a way that is intentional and relies on the Holy Spirit.

When you think about your spiritual life, is there something else you are hoping to discover? What are you wrestling with? What are you curious about? Do your best to define the question you are truly asking in this season. Next, be sure to engage the ideation process! Spirituality is one of the areas of life we can easily box in. I love the book *Sacred Pathways* by Gary Thomas.[5] He outlines the many ways that people connect with God. Many of us can get stuck in a rut, assuming that there are only a couple of ways to connect with God, and if we are feeling estranged from God, we keep doing what we've always done and hope something changes eventually.

Thomas gives the profiles of nine different types of people who may find their most direct, sacred pathways to God in very different ways. There are the naturalists, who love God through nature; the sensates, who love God through the senses; the traditionalists, who love God through ritual and symbol; the ascetics, who love God through solitude and simplicity; the activists, who love God through confrontation and active change-making; the caregivers, who love God through caring for others' needs; the enthusiasts, who love God with mystery and celebration; the contemplatives, who love God through adoration; and finally, the intellectuals, who love God with their minds.

I share these nine pathways with you because they could help give you ideas for what your first experiment may be. For instance, if you realize that the intellectual pathway is a way you can connect with God, then you may choose to read commentaries along with the Bible instead of a devotional book. If you notice you connect with God through the senses, then you may create a space in your home with scented candles or some beautiful art where you can sit and pray. What is the question you are trying to answer, the decision you are trying to make, or the problem you are trying to solve? Do these pathways hold clues for your next step? If the first experiment you think of is too lofty, break it down and consider if there is a simpler initial experiment to help get you going.

CASE STUDIES

Once you determine your experiment, you need to do the intentional work of breaking it down into steps. Below I offer a couple of case studies that can help give you guidance for your specific experiment. One of these may resonate with you, but you will need to design your own experiment!

Case Study 1

Joel had felt like God was far away for a long time. Jesus seemed like an old friend whom he had lost touch with rather than a good friend he did life with. He couldn't remember a time when God had felt near. After listening, discussing, and creating space for ideating, he determined that his spiritual life question was "How can I experience God as truly *with* me?"

    He settled on his first experiment. He would create a detailed spiritual timeline as he looked back on his life and see what he might learn. Would he find any patterns or themes? He hoped he would discover something that would lead him to the next experiment so that he could experience God again as near to him in his life.

    He outlined the detailed steps:

Step 1: He selected a time in his calendar to sit down and process. He saved the date so he wouldn't forget or double-book.

Step 2: He gathered the materials he needed. Joel is a pretty artistic guy, so he thought a large piece of poster board cut in two would create a long timeline, leaving space for him to not only write words but also draw any pictures or images. He also bought some brand-new colored pencils. He knew those would entice him to keep his commitment to himself to try this experiment.

Step 3: He shared with his wife that he was going to take time to write out his spiritual timeline. This created built-in accountability. She was also able to give him uninterrupted space on a Thursday night.

Step 4: He asked his wife if she would be willing on their next date night to help him review what he learned from the experiment. She was happy to reserve a date night for that as long as it also included their favorite takeout.

Step 5: He got settled with his pencils, said a short prayer asking God to help reveal what God wanted to show him, and wrote out his life story from a spiritual perspective.

After the experiment and processing with his wife, Joel realized he had learned a lot about himself and how God had interacted with him over the years. He also noticed something important: he felt closest to God when he and a mentor or a couple of other friends met regularly to discuss their spiritual lives. They would ask each other how they were experiencing God and what God might be doing in their lives. This made sense to him because he was outgoing and extroverted and could get stuck in his head without space to verbally process. He also realized he was relying on his wife to be his only outlet for discussing all of the deep aspects of life, and perhaps others needed to be a part of that process as well. So for his next experiment, he was going to design a way of identifying others whom he could connect with regularly and intentionally. He set a time to write out the detailed steps to that next experiment.

Case Study 2

Sarah had not felt at home in her faith community for a while. She wasn't sure what was making her uncomfortable, but she knew it had to do with some comments she had heard staff members make regarding the co-lead pastors, who were husband and wife. She decided an experiment would be to have intentional conversations with those who had made the comments as well as with the lead pastors, if they were willing. After that experiment, she came away feeling as though something was going on that the staff members and the pastors weren't being honest about.

This left Sarah with the heartbreaking decision to look for a different church home. She never expected to make a change, but the growing feeling that something toxic was happening and the lack of willingness to talk about it when she confronted the leaders caused her to feel as though she had no choice. She had only "church shopped" once before, and it always felt cringy—like she was trying to pick out a new car at a dealership or weighing the pros and cons as though she was an analyst for *Consumer Reports*. This dread prevented her from going to any worship services or joining in any faith community at all.

After a few months, the news hit Facebook that the co-pastors were leaving her former church because they had been concealing an affair one of those pastors had been having with a congregation member for years. Sarah brought this up with her therapist, and it was an area of focus for a few weeks. They both agreed that going back to her church was not a healthy option for her if she wanted to grow spiritually. They also decided that it was time for her to make a move and begin searching for a community she could trust before she gave up on the idea completely.

She defined her question as "Is there a faith community where I can feel at home?" After some prayer and listening to God, she committed to some factors that were necessary for her. She sought a healthy faith community led by healthy leadership where the focus was on Jesus but it was OK to have diversity of thought and experience. She also wanted a church that tries to live out actively what they talked about. She knew that these traits were more important than the music style or the programs. She also realized she hoped to find a community where she could really commit and see herself there indefinitely. In the meantime, though, she had the freedom to experience different communities. Perhaps this experiment could also teach her about the breadth of the Christian church, since she was in a time of her life when she was free to try different expressions. So she designed an experiment to take two months to experience a wide range of church communities.

Step 1: Sarah made a list of churches to attend for worship, spanning a variety of ethnic backgrounds (including multiethnic churches) and those that were more liturgical, charismatic, and multigenerational and from different denominations.

Step 2: She had a friend whose little church had just closed, so she asked her friend if she would be interested in joining in this experiment. She said yes, and that made the experiment a million times easier, since Sarah wouldn't need to go to these churches alone.

Step 3: She put in her calendar the first two months of the churches she would visit.

Step 4: She selected a journal where she would process each experience after talking with her friend about it after lunch. She wrote what resonated with her and what didn't. She asked God to bring to the surface what she should notice about each church, and she added these observations to her journal.

Step 5: She put a date in the calendar for her and her friend to talk through their experiences and what they had learned after the two months.

After the experiment, they found that one of the churches they had visited on the third week really resonated with them. They watched a few more of their services online and decided the next experiment would be to go to that church for a few weeks in a row, keeping the important factors they named at the forefront.

Check out the Decision-Making Toolbox in the appendix for tools to help you in designing your spiritual life experiments as well as making other decisions regarding faith and God.

10

PURPOSE AND MISSION EXPERIMENTS

*Experiments for joining God's mission and living
more fully into God's purpose for your life.*

I looked down at the notes in my hand. When I had prepared this outline for the discipleship group I was leading, I felt it was going to be pretty meaningful for the women who gathered. Feeling perhaps a little too proud of myself, I was caught off guard by the way the conversation started before we had even officially begun the organized group time. A couple of the women confessed a lack of fulfillment in their lives. As I listened, I set the planned outline off to the side, feeling a question rising in my mind and heart.

"What would you do next if you had no fear?" I lobbed the question out into the room without even formally starting the group time. After a few blinks and a little bit of nervous laughter, I said, "I'm serious. Let's all go around and share. It doesn't mean we are on the hook for anything. Let's just try to share as authentically as possible."

Two hours later, there had been tears, more nervous laughter, a lot of fears named, significant affirmation offered to one another, and more than a couple experiments on their way to being designed and implemented. The question God gave me for that conversation was key, but what I didn't realize was how important it was to name our fears as well. Psychologist Dan Siegel coined the phrase "name it to tame it" in his book about child development.[1] When kids are having big emotions, it's helpful to come alongside them and help them name what they are feeling. When they do, they can tame or calm down the part of their brain experiencing an emotional overload. I have found this works for adults as well. When the women had the courage to name the fears they were experiencing, the fear had less power over them. And when their fears had less power, they were able to see their true purpose and mission more clearly.

I don't remember all that was said that day, but I remember my friend Tanya said she would start a missional community focused on bridge-building with the Latino community. This was a passion of hers, as she was Latina herself and could see how often these folks felt like outsiders and experienced barriers those in the majority culture did not have to overcome. She did start that group! They were instrumental in helping communicate during a housing crisis in our city because they followed God into this adventure.

My friend Steph shared that she and her husband, who were both actors, had always dreamed of leaving Minnesota and seeing if they could make it in New York City. A few months after that group conversation, they packed up their car and drove east. To be honest, they didn't end up having the experience of acting as they had hoped; instead, they ended up as part of a team that planted a church in Brooklyn that loves their community in the name of Jesus. They also had two beautiful little girls. This reminds me of the story of Paul's vision in Acts 16, where the vision helped them make the move, but God had something else in mind.

One of the most emotional stories we heard during that group time was from Alissa, whose house we were meeting at. She was in her thirties, had bought a house as a single woman, and had been doing well in her career, but something huge was on her heart. When she was growing up, her parents had adopted children from Romania and Russia who became her siblings. This resulted in her whole family spending time in Romania while she was growing up. She had seen firsthand the many children orphaned and longed to adopt as her parents had. However, the government of Romania had halted all overseas adoptions indefinitely.

"If I weren't afraid, I would move to Romania and become a house mom at an orphanage," she stated through tears. Alissa has spent the last six years in Romania living as a house mom just like she boldly declared that day. She is working on her residency and is currently raising money to buy a house so she can adopt children in the future. Dozens of kids have been in her care and will continue to be as she lives out her calling and purpose.

For most of us, our purpose and mission won't mean moving across the country or the world, but if we want to live lives of meaning, we will need to make a move. We will need to experiment our way into the places, spaces, and relationships God will lead us to if we are paying attention.

FOLLOW THE RIGHT FLAGS

A couple of years ago, my church joined in a 6K run to raise money for clean water for kids in the developing world. Six kilometers is the average distance kids and women need to walk to get water in many parts of the world.[2] Oftentimes, the water they carry home isn't even clean but is full of contaminants. The race organizers had placed orange flags throughout the city park system so we could follow the route that would lead us back to where we started.

About halfway through the race, the two others I was jogging with noticed something was off. We looked around, and those running with us were not from the same 6K group we had started with. It turns out there was another run that same morning, and the courses intersected. The organizers from that race also used orange flags! We eventually made our way back to the correct course, but we did end up running, or jogging, more than a 6K that day.

This is often how we experience purpose in our lives. We have a sense that God may want us to join in an area of mission, and we may even set out to run that race. But we easily lose track of the course and find ourselves running off in the wrong direction. Just like me and my friends, if we notice we are off course and not making progress in what we had set out to do, we have a chance to stop and get back on track. Hebrews 12:1–3 has become very well known for this very image of running a race. I love how Eugene Peterson puts it in The Message translation:

> Strip down, start running—and never quit! No extra spiritual fat, no parasitic sins. Keep your eyes on *Jesus*, who both began and finished this race we're in. Study how he did it. Because he never lost sight of where he was headed—that exhilarating finish in and with God—he could put up with anything along the way: Cross, shame, whatever. And now he's *there*, in the place of honor, right alongside God. When you find yourselves flagging in your faith, go over that story again, item by item, that long litany of hostility he plowed through. *That* will shoot adrenaline into your souls!

I want to name some of the barriers we face when it comes to running the race God asks us to join in God's mission of love and redemption in the world. I do this not to shame anyone but because being blind to these barriers can keep us from experiencing the fulfillment that comes from running. Or they can cause us not to see progress, since we aren't making it past the mile markers telling us just how far we've come.

BARRIERS TO RUNNING THE RACE OF PURPOSE

Getting off course is certainly a barrier to running our race. There are a few reasons we get off course when it comes to discovering and staying in step with our purpose. In my story, we weren't following the right flags—we got distracted and didn't realize we weren't following the same orange flags from the first half of the race. Distractions in our lives often get us off course from our purpose. Think about something you felt deeply passionate about in the past—was there a distraction that led you off course? I know for me that relationships, busyness, and other daily realities have distracted me from the purpose I knew I wanted to follow in my life.

Another way to get off course is by pursuing what at first seems like a good thing but is actually a distraction from a deeper purpose. A great example of this is the very popular happiness movement. There are journals and books and motivational talks and gatherings that can help you pursue happiness in your life. While I see why this is so tempting, happiness alone is not a fulfilling way to live. It wears out quickly! It is one of those flags that looks like it is on the course of purpose but instead takes us off course.

We can also get off course if we are nearsighted. As I mentioned earlier, I am physically nearsighted, and I can't see very far out in front of me before things get pretty blurry. I think most of us are spiritually nearsighted, meaning we tend to only observe what is right around us. We don't naturally look for realities that don't directly affect us or the people we are close to. This is the reason that dominant North American culture is so deeply individualistic and struggles with selfishness and self-preservation. So many of us want to make a difference in the world around us, but at the end of the day, we are spiritually nearsighted and don't see what we aren't looking for. It's another reason we may metaphorically miss our flags and run off course.

When God opens our eyes to things in the world around us, it's like when I got corrective lenses for the first time in second grade. Now I can't imagine seeing without my glasses! How could I stand being so nearsighted? Once I saw more clearly, I didn't want to go back. But the truth is, I didn't wear my glasses consistently for a few years because I was embarrassed to be one of the only kids wearing glasses at school. This meant I missed a lot of the big picture of what was happening around me until fifth or sixth grade. I couldn't see the blackboard, and I still think this is why I'm so terrible at my times tables from third grade!

There are times in life when we are given the chance to look through corrective lenses, so to speak. May 2020 was one of those times. A few miles from my house, George Floyd, a Black man, was murdered by a white Minneapolis police officer, and all eight brutal minutes of it were recorded as clear as day on a cell phone video. It sparked a worldwide race revolution and the largest protest in history. It was an opportunity of reckoning for any of us who had been too nearsighted to see how police brutality and many other aspects of systemic racism had been devastating our Black brothers and sisters, as well as other Indigenous people and people of color, for hundreds of years. I and other white people like me heard a plea from our BIPOC friends, asking us to let this lead to permanent change—not to go back to our nearsightedness but to keep our corrective lenses on even when others refused to wear them. Just like little second-grade Steph, will we choose to wear our corrective lenses even when it's not popular or when we feel singled out for refusing to go back to the nearsightedness that harmed our brothers and sisters?

This brings up the barrier of complacency. The tough reality is that the pull toward complacency is often much stronger than the pull toward compassion. Jesus teaches us that the most important things we can do in life are to love God and love our neighbor as ourselves. But I know I have experienced the weight of complacency holding me back from loving God well, certainly from loving my neighbor well, and even from having compassion for myself so I can love myself well. And if I don't have a healthy sense of compassion and love for myself, no wonder I run out of steam to love God and neighbor.

Peterson's translation of Hebrews 12:1 says, "Strip down, start running—and never quit!"[3] Complacency is one of the things that we need to strip off. Our love of comfort is so strong, and we sink into it so easily. To have compassion is to let our hearts break for what breaks the heart of God. This is a nice concept in theory, but in actuality, it is a very heavy experience. It often leads us to what many have called compassion fatigue. We can get so weighed down by the pain and suffering in the world that perhaps we don't run off course, but we just stop running altogether. The many deep needs in the world can result in an inability to take a step toward any of them. Just like the jam experiment I talked about in chapter 8, we can find ourselves in decision paralysis and fail to take any steps to join in God's mission.

Some of us mask this reality through what I call "slactivism"—we post on social media as though we are trying to do something about these problems, but we don't actually take action. Yes, being vocal about matters of injustice does matter; we just need to be sure it isn't masking a lack of action toward joining in the restoration of God in these areas.

MARATHONS WITH HURDLES

Now that we have named the barriers, let's talk about how they don't need to slow us down or hold us back! Perhaps we should admit that the race we are running is not a 6K but rather a marathon. It's lifelong! So if we get off course, that's OK; the important thing is that we find our way back.

We also could think of this race as a marathon that has a section of hurdles every once in a while. I remember watching steeplechase for the first time—an Olympic sport where the runners have to jump hurdles and other obstacles as they make their way through a course of sorts. A typical three-thousand-meter steeplechase course has twenty-eight barriers and seven water jumps. If you've never watched it, head to YouTube right away! Then imagine that a marathon and steeplechase had a baby—that's life on mission. When we come to expect hurdles or water jumps, we will be able to be ready for them.

To survive this race, we need to build our endurance so that we don't give in to complacency and compassion fatigue. We have to remember a few things that can help us avoid getting worn down and worn out too quickly. First of all, we're not called to every area of need all at once. The famous quote from Frederick Buechner helps us recognize this: "The place God calls you to is the place where your deep gladness and the world's deep hunger meet."[4]

Notice the quote is not "God calls you to every place you can possibly get to, to do whatever you can do, no matter if you are made for it or not, because the world has a lot of deep hunger." Yet so many of us act as though this is the case. Here's another one of those dreaded road analogies of mine: You are running this race, and there is a ditch on one side that is apathy and a lack of caring altogether, but the overcorrection to the other side is thinking you have to care about everything equally and fully, thus causing burnout.

Both ditches get us off track. Listening and then experimenting in this area of life is critical because it helps us start responding instead of merely reacting. Sometimes we need to react quickly, but most of the time, thoughtfulness and discernment will get us on track in the direction we are supposed to be running.

ONE MARKER AT A TIME

There is a lot to juggle in life, with our careers, paying the bills, and taking care of our own needs and perhaps the needs of children or an aging parent. Where is there time for mission? Of course, this is a struggle that many face; you are not alone. We need to run this race just one marker at a time. When I am out jogging, I look off into the distance, pick a tree or a bend in the road, and fix my eyes on that so I can just think about making it that far. Hebrews invites us to keep our eyes fixed on Jesus, who is the leader of this race. Jesus is the one who can help us see that we just need to take it one day and one step at a time. Have you asked him for help? I believe he is ready to jog with you every step of the way.

In order to create clear steps for the experiments of purpose and mission, we may need to make some space in our lives. Do you need to let go of some things? Groups you are a part of that have for a long time zapped your energy? An extra committee at work that you really don't need to be on? Have you let your Netflix hobby take over just a bit too much? Are the kids in just a few too many extracurricular activities, even for their own good?

Many of us have to stop and acknowledge the reality that our hearts are often bigger than our calendars. Depending on your personality, a full calendar may indicate an overstuffed mind and heart! If we don't prioritize purpose, we will never find it. If you have little ones, they too can be a part of the purpose—it just may mean being creative! Watching you living into your purpose could become one of the most important things they learn.

Finally, mission and purpose have a way of not just adding to our lives but in many ways changing how we see what we are already doing. As you think about an experiment you may want to try, consider how the steps may fit right into what you are already doing in your life. I'll flesh this out in the following case studies to awaken your missional imagination to how purpose and meaning may not be all that far off!

CASE STUDIES

Once you determine your experiment, you'll need to intentionally break it down into steps. I will give you a few case studies that can help give you guidance for your specific experiment. One of these may resonate with you, but don't be afraid to design your own experiment!

Case Study 1

Juanita had been learning about the concept of neighboring from a friend who had read a book on the subject. "I am realizing that we can't love our neighbors as Jesus tells us to if we don't even know their names!" her friend shared over drinks at happy hour. This inspired Juanita to ask herself what it would mean to love her actual geographical neighbors. She had lived in her neighborhood for a few years and knew a few people's names, but she realized she tended to drive into her garage and enter her house without seeing anyone, and her neighbors did the same. "I'm going to need to try something different if I am going to actually meet these folks," she thought to herself. When she prayed about this, God brought to her mind that some of her neighbors might live alone and experience deep loneliness because they didn't have a community like she did.

She began to design an initial experiment in order to move forward in being a good neighbor so she could experience purpose right where she was living!

Step 1: Juanita drew a small map of the few blocks around her house and the corresponding house numbers. She wrote "Neighbors Names" on the map and attached it to her fridge.

Step 2: She made a plan to walk around her neighborhood more frequently. She determined she could do this at least three times a week for the month of June.

Step 3: She wrote out the script she would use if she saw a neighbor: *Hi! I live at 1365 Rose Street, and I am trying to learn more neighbors' names this summer. I'm Juanita. What's your name?*

Step 4: She began her walks without earbuds in to pray for her neighborhood by paying attention to what she saw around her. When something resonated with her, she began to pray about what came to mind.

Step 5: When she saw a neighbor, she approached, started with her script, and let the conversation go naturally. Sometimes the conversation fizzled out, but other times she got their names and continued the conversation.

Step 6: She created a note in her phone where she recorded the name and house number of the neighbor she met and then added it to the list on the fridge when she got home.

Step 7: When she passed her fridge, she offered a prayer for one neighbor whose name jumped out at her.

Step 8: She made a plan with her friend to review this experiment at the end of June at another happy hour.

After a month of trying this experiment, Juanita had met twenty-seven neighbors! She had begun to have regular conversations with three or four who spent more time in their front yards than others and who had seemed the most open to getting to know her. Her next experiment was to host a simple "front-yard" party at her house, inviting people to bring their favorite summer snack and a chair, and she would provide water and lemonade. She made some small invitations and went from house to house, even stopping at those neighbors' homes whom she hadn't yet met. She learned even more names, and those who came to the front-yard party lingered longer than she had expected!

Case Study 2

Jordan had watched a short documentary called *Uganda Gold*, which revealed the heartbreaking realities of the water crisis in that country and much of the developing world. (While these case studies are fictional, my husband really did produce this documentary, and you can watch it on Amazon Prime!) Even though days went by, images kept flashing through his mind of the joy on the faces of those who were pumping clear water for the first time in their village. "I don't think I will ever go to Africa, but perhaps there is something I could do from here," he wondered. Since he had an eleven-year-old daughter, he was especially heartbroken for how the lack of clear water affects the young girls, causing them to drop out of school, fall prey to sexual violence at a young age, and often experience unwanted teenage pregnancy.

Jordan had a lot on his plate. He had just been promoted at work and now had direct reports for the first time. He had to learn quickly how to be a good manager. Besides the many other obligations and commitments to his family and church, he also had been convinced to coach his daughter's soccer team again this fall. He loved her, but that many eleven-year-old girls was a lot for anyone! That's when it hit him: What if the soccer team could be a part of making a difference on the other side of the world? What if the team could help raise the funds to build a well? How cool would it be to see these young girls come to understand what their Ugandan sisters were experiencing? He brought the idea up to his wife and the assistant coach and then began to design the experiment.

Step 1: They sent an email to the other parents, sharing the idea and a link to the documentary. They asked the parents if they would support the idea of the team making a plan to raise some funds to build a well in Uganda. "Please don't feel obligated, but if anyone wants to be a part of leading the girls in this, please let us know," they added at the end of the email. They got a thumbs-up from all the parents and a couple who said they'd love to help.

Step 2: They planned a night to watch the film with the girls and wrote out two or three questions to lead a discussion of what they had seen.

Step 3: They pitched the idea to the girls of how their team could be a part of raising money for a well. They led them through a brainstorming session for how they could do this.

Step 4: The adult leaders looked over the ideas and helped choose the most realistic option.

Step 5: They helped the girls launch their fundraiser.

Of course, this initial experiment quickly resulted in a fundraiser, which was an experiment in itself. At first, they discussed a car wash idea, but it seemed like the amount of water they would likely waste in that process could send the wrong message. Since some were Girl Scouts, they proposed selling cookies or other items as well. Eventually, the parents helped guide them back to how they could use their skills as soccer players. The final result was that the girls got T-shirts as well as new jerseys that said, "We win for water." They then committed to asking people in their lives if they would give $5, $50, or $500 if they could win 50 percent of their games that season. In the end, the girls did win half their games and raised almost $5,000, which is halfway to the cost of a well for a village of three hundred people! The girls were determined to get the other half the following season. While the families of the team came from all sorts of faith backgrounds, Jordan talked with his daughter about how God's heart for the people of Uganda was the same as God's heart for the people of America. They committed to praying that God would lead them as they cared for what God cares about around the world and right in their own city.[5]

Check out the Decision-Making Toolbox in the appendix for tools to help you in designing your purpose and mission experiments as well as making other decisions.

11

VOCATIONAL EXPERIMENTS

*Experiments about work and how to make
a living while still having a life.*

"So you're sure I've never met her before?" I asked my mom on the phone, calling from my dorm room. My mom had sent a package to me at college that included some mail that had been delivered at home, and inside was a postcard from a woman I had never met. She was on my mom's Christmas card list, and each Christmas, my mom had written a little paragraph about what I was up to. As far as we knew, all she knew about me came from the few sentences in those Christmas cards.

She wrote, "Steph, will you consider becoming a pastor? You certainly display the gifts we look for to challenge someone to go to seminary! With love, Marianne." On the back was a photo of Marianne wearing a clerical collar, so it seemed she was a pastor herself. As a twenty-one-year-old with very little experience beyond my own faith tradition, this photo seemed unusual on so many levels. First of all, I had rarely seen a pastor with a clerical collar. Also, I could count on one hand how many women pastors I had met. That day, I began taking steps toward what I felt then and still feel today is my calling—to be a pastor.

Now, I realize I was young—very few people know what they are called to do at the age of twenty-one. For that I truly am thankful. But before you get the idea that all it took was a post-card to know what I was supposed to do with my life, let me give you a little more context. I had six other pastors ask me a question similar to Marianne's; the first time was when I was only fifteen. For the next six years, I thought about pretty much every other option available to me as a future vocation.

It wasn't that I was running from the idea or that I was even all that reluctant. It's just that vocational questions are so difficult for most of us, and I wasn't an exception. Also, my lack of experience caused me to assume that these folks must be mistaken—generally, people of my gender, personality type, and passion areas weren't pastors in churches. When I look with broad strokes at my colleagues today, I might still be considered a bit of an outlier, but that doesn't automatically mean this vocation isn't right for me. It just created multiple hurdles that others didn't have to jump over to figure out the best profession. Back to the steeplechase analogy again!

It may seem like seven people bringing up the same vocation would make it obvious, but until that postcard from Marianne, it really didn't feel like it. That postcard helped me connect these conversations as something the Holy Spirit was prompting. With hindsight bias, I can see how God was using this pattern and these people to guide me. But when we are wondering and questioning our vocational options, it can feel like we are deep in the weeds and can't see our way out.

Almost twenty years later, I am still primarily living into the vocational calling to be a pastor, but along the way, there have been many other questions. The concept of vocation for most of us is not merely our job but how we will use all of our time and energy. I tend to think of a vocation as the roles and work that one participates in that contribute to the greater good of society and support their and/or their family's livelihood.

My definition of *vocation*, then, would include caring for children and aging adults and performing volunteer work or other endeavors in which you don't receive monetary payment. It would also include what sociologist Micaela di Leonardo calls "kin work," the work done to hold relational webs of family and community together.[1] This work can be as demanding as a full-time job (or more demanding for many folks) and is typically unpaid. Of course, even today much of this work is done by women, although not exclusively. Many men have found it meaningful and enjoyable to join in this work, and you can see how families who share this work can experience a deeper partnership.

Vocation in my perspective also includes learning, both formal and informal education. Many folks have a paid job and are also part-time or even full-time students—both their job and their studies are part of their vocation. Finally, when someone is looking for work or discerning a change in their vocation, that discernment work itself is also an aspect of their vocation!

So for me, as I write this, I see my paid vocation including being a pastor, professor, leadership coach, and author. However, I also add to my vocation the work I do producing podcasts; even though this is not a paid endeavor, I see it as contributing to the greater good. Time that I volunteer in my neighborhood and for those in need in my city and community is also part of my vocation. Finally, being a good wife, sister, daughter, aunt, and friend are all critical aspects of my vocation. I give a lot of my time as well as emotional and mental energy to keeping my family and communities connected relationally. While we will talk specifically about relational experiments in the next chapter, I have found it helpful to see this "work" as a part of vocation rather than compartmentalizing kin work as something else.

Thinking about vocation through this big-picture approach is helpful as we talk about designing experiments for vocational decisions. It can be a trap to think about your vocation as merely what you get paid to do. Experiments that transcend merely what we see as our paid profession will lead to deeper purpose and meaning in the work we do in our lives. When we integrate the concept of vocation, it can help us recognize the mental load that comes from not only the work we get paid to do but the kin work many do daily, as well as the discernment work we do when a career change may be up ahead. It can empower us to see learning and education as critical parts of vocation— even though we rarely get paid to learn and often are the ones paying to get the education!

LOGISTICS—WHAT DOES THAT EVEN MEAN?

My brother, Rob, had just moved back to Minnesota with his wife of three years, they were in their midtwenties, and both were knee-deep into their first professional roles. My brother had a disappointing experience working for a nonprofit—sitting at a desk, sending emails, and making phone calls all day long, he was withering on the vine. When he moved back, he found out that his alma mater offered free career assessments for their alums. (*Tip:* This could be a great part of the listening process for anyone considering a vocational experiment. See if you have access to a skills test or assessment for free or a small fee with a career counselor!)

When Rob got his results, he was confused at first. "Logistics" came up as one of his top career field options. Initially, he had no idea what that meant, but he soon realized that these were the folks who did things like help the soap or cereal companies get their products to the various big-box stores. Feeling a crunch for time, he hopped on LinkedIn and found another alum from our college who had this listed as their field. He was connected from one person to the next, from one informational interview to another. He felt as though he was a hot potato being passed around. This is often how networking feels in the middle of it! Finally, he landed an entry-level job at a logistics firm that helped sort out the details for products to move to Minnesota-based companies like Target and General Mills.

I came to visit him on site at the General Mills campus, ate at their fancy cafeteria, and listened to him talk about his job. He had an energy I hadn't seen in a while, as he was finally using his brain as it was wired, and that was clearly life-giving to him. But as he talked, I could tell something was missing. When he was a teenager, I remember him saying, "I don't know what I want to do with my life, but I know I want to help people." Something in me felt like helping the right amount of Cheerios get to the right Target was not the kind of helping that he felt created to do. When my church had an opportunity to help with a problem at our local school, we realized quickly it needed some logistical experience, so of course Rob jumped in, ready to help!

Seeing his vocation as more than what he got paid to do permitted him to pour his free time into this project. You see, the school where we worship had shared with us a growing problem they were facing with their students. Since there was such a high rate of poverty among the kids' families, the kids were stealing food or taking it out of the trash on Fridays because they were facing food insecurity at home on the weekends. It was such a heartbreaking reality that we knew we needed to help. Rob had the skills to make it possible for our little community to make a big impact. With his help, we were able to offer a bag of food for every kid in our school whose family requested one by discreetly placing it in their backpack on Friday before they went home for the weekend. By the end of the year, that was almost three hundred kids!

TO JOB SEARCH OR NOT TO JOB SEARCH?

It didn't take a change of career for Rob to do what he felt wired to do with his paid vocation and also with the gift of his time to the community. If you feel like your mind and heart are engaged in the work you get paid to do, that is a gift. Job satisfaction is not very high overall. I've heard job coaches suggest that only 20 percent of people like 80 percent of their job. And thus 80 percent of people dislike much or most of their job. When it comes to vocational experiments, many of you might consider whether you need to change your paid vocation or if you can be fulfilled by giving some of your free time to projects or roles that allow you to contribute to the greater good without making a career change.

For others, your experiments may lead you to a very significant change. Either way, I offer you this challenge: before you start the process or the experiments to switch careers, examine what you are doing currently. Whether you are in middle management at a company or slinging lattes at a coffee shop, look for ways your current job can contribute to human flourishing. We are created with the ability to bear the image of God in all sorts of work. It is a real shame that some people of faith have created a hierarchy when it comes to "God's work."

Maybe you have heard these types of assumptions. Those called to ministry or missions are clearly the most honored by God. Next, we have helping professions and education. Somewhere in there, we can put other helpful services, like transportation, communication, and even some other roles like electricians and plumbers. But at the bottom of the "righteous calling hierarchy," we have businesspeople, salespeople, and other seemingly profit-driven endeavors. But don't worry, you can redeem the lack of holiness in your career by giving a good portion of your hard-earned money away! People in roles like mine may then also add, "The most important part of your job is sharing your faith with your coworkers and inviting them to church."

If that doesn't sound familiar to you, then I am glad! But the cultures I have been in most of my life have created a deeply embarrassing and disappointing false hierarchy. You can bear the image of God in any career! When you follow God into a vocation that is good for you, that calling is just as important as any other, including vocational ministry. I'm so sorry if you have felt belittled or minimized in your role, or if you have been made to feel like your best contribution is the financial support of churches or nonprofits. Also, it is wonderful to consider how your coworkers are your work neighbors and how you might love them as yourself, as Jesus commanded us to do. It's great if you have opportunities to share your faith with them, but your witness, as we sometimes call it, will be much stronger if you also do your job well and commit yourself to being the best version of yourself while fulfilling your job description.

In addition to loving your work neighbors and making money that you can be generous with, there are three other ways your work matters to God. First, God can use your vocation, paid or otherwise, to form you spiritually. Don't buy into the illusion that a church program or some sort of faith-based book group is the only way to grow in faith. You spend most of your waking hours at work or living into your broader vocation. Try asking Jesus to show you how your work can form you to be more like him on a daily basis.

Second, God can use you in your workplace to be a person of integrity. Many times, we wonder if a decision our company or organization is making is ethical, moral, or truly about the flourishing of all people. We have the opportunity to advocate for equity, honesty, and social concern in our workplaces. This can be difficult, but God gives us wisdom and courage. And this work is not only needed in for-profit companies. Nonprofits with missions of justice, as well as churches and Christian organizations, are just as capable of making mistakes that are harmful and unethical and contribute to the tearing down of individuals and groups of people. Ask God's Spirit to show you how you can use your voice and your role to speak for those who are not being heard or to shed light on an area that doesn't serve the greater good of humanity—or your organization, for that matter.

Finally, we all have an opportunity to see the way that we bear God's image through our work. I believe in the core theological concept that stems from Genesis 1 that humans were made in the image of God.[2] Thus the way we live our lives, including our work, resembles who God is and what God does. Think about the job (or jobs) you have right now—no matter what it is, you have the opportunity to bear God's image. Whenever I talk about this, people bring up work that is illegal or immoral in their minds. Sure, there are limits, but my point is, most of the time we tend to shrink the roles that resemble and bear the image of God to just a short list.

For instance, in the false career hierarchy I described earlier, the service industry is usually placed in the middle at best or at the bottom at worst. But during the global pandemic, we came to realize just how much human flourishing relies on the many facets of the service industry. This industry holds together the relational, as well as economic, threads of society. We were not a great version of ourselves when we were without these important workers. The way those in the service industry provide for others and create space for hospitality resembles God's provision and deep welcome to humanity through creation.

Take a look at this list that describes the value of work, and think about the job you have right now, or maybe your last few jobs. Every one of these activities bears the image of God. My challenge to you is to find a job that doesn't have at least one of these qualities—I doubt you will find one!

- create organization from chaos
- sustain or produce resources that help people thrive
- organize spaces necessary or helpful for people to thrive
- infuse hope in the midst of struggle or suffering
- bring life, care for life, or sustain life
- care for the natural world and its resources
- bring beauty or creativity
- tell or share stories
- help people learn and receive resources for thriving
- help people understand their purpose or story
- help people overcome barriers to living their best lives
- support, coach, or develop people or coworkers
- offer food or nourishment to support human flourishing
- foster relationships and communication between people
- help people rest or create spaces for recreation

Before you start experimenting for a change, take some time to evaluate your work through this framework. I have noticed that those who can't find any inherent value in a career or role they don't love continue to struggle even after making a switch.

HOW DID YOU GET HERE?

Those of you considering an experiment to make a change or decision about your vocation have gotten to this point in any number of ways. Some of you may be in the early stages of discovering what your first career may be. This is a great time to experiment! In his early twenties, my husband realized he was interested in three different careers. He did three six- to nine-month experiments. The third one led him to filmmaking and videography, and that has been his career ever since. He loves it!

Some of you are thinking about experimenting vocationally because you have recently lost your job. This can be so difficult and often unexpected. Many times, grief is an important precursor to an experiment; it can actually be an important part of the process of moving forward. Some of you are wondering about vocation because you have a sense of unsettledness or you are starting to realize that you lack fulfillment in your job or career.

Remember to think about the big picture of vocation so you don't make a job switch that doesn't offer much more fulfillment. However, when you have a feeling of uneasiness about your vocation that you just can't shake, experimenting is a great way to take steps without jumping into the deep end and potentially making too big of a change too fast. Change is always risky, but when it comes to the work that provides our income—especially if we have a partner or others we help provide for—the risk goes beyond just ourselves.

One note about the lack of fulfillment many of us feel even when we find a career or vocation we love: We are humans living in a world that has many wonderful attributes but is not as it should be. It's wonderful to appreciate your big-picture vocation as a worker, friend, parent, volunteer, and so on. We can experience so much joy from these roles and activities. But we all experience disappointment and often pain in these areas as well. No job, combination of jobs, or vocation is perfect, because we don't live in a perfect world.

Our future hope is that Jesus will return to restore the world to all its potential and more. So if you find yourself with a consistent sense of longing, I think it's normal to long for that future. Longing is what hope looks like on a hard day. The quest to satiate that longing in this life can become exhausting, like chasing down something that can never be caught. However, there *is* something more than what we experience now. This future hope is important to keep in mind, as job searches and constant transition can often run us ragged.

WHEN A BIG CHANGE IS COMING

What my brother, Rob, didn't realize was that this new volunteer role helping to feed kids in the public school where our church met was only the beginning. This was such a meaningful and exciting process that he began to wonder if there was something more for him in this. Rob reached out to a couple of other churches and asked if he could help them do the same thing at the schools they were partnering with. They were eager to join in because the local schools they partnered with had students who were facing the same food insecurity struggle.

A Bible study group at our church was reading Numbers 13–14, about the spies who went to scope out the land God had promised to God's people. If you know the story, you know that the people there were big and powerful, so God's people were full of fear. That Scripture reading flipped a switch in Rob's mind and heart, and he began to pursue what it would look like to take a risk and launch a nonprofit that could provide logistics so that no kid in Minnesota schools would go hungry over the weekend. He felt like giants were in the way, just like in the Bible story, but he felt compelled to try anyway.

He raised some money and then resigned from his logistics company to this venture. His boss was proud of him but offered to let him work part-time at first, even though that was unusual at the company. Within ten months, Rob's new nonprofit was scaling to the point that he had to work at it full-time and, a few months later, add some part-time staff. The nonprofit is named "Every Meal," because every child should have access to every meal and never wonder where their next meal will come from.

Every Meal now has over 250 community groups and churches sponsoring over 270 schools in Minnesota. They led one of the largest efforts to provide food to kids and families in Minneapolis during the COVID-19 pandemic as well as after the uprising resulting from the murder of George Floyd. They have provided over six million meals to families in Minnesota.

But it all started with an experiment. Rob's questions led from one experiment to the next: "What if I took a skills inventory? What if I put time and effort into networking? What if I can use logistics outside of my paid position to make a difference? What if we tried to help more schools? What if I raised money and tried to scale this effort even further?" Question, experiment, question, experiment. It all resulted in millions of meals for kids in need.

Now, what is your "What if?" that can get you started experimenting in your vocational next steps?

CASE STUDIES

Case Study 1

Lindsey and Raul had been married for six years and had a nine-month-old and a four-year-old. Lindsey took time off for both kids when they were born before heading back to her job as a first-grade teacher. She loved teaching, but each transition back from maternity leave triggered a nagging feeling in her heart. She didn't want to be a stay-at-home parent, even though there would be some great aspects to that; besides, they couldn't afford it. She found herself dreaming about starting a small childcare center that could focus on kindergarten readiness at an afford-able rate for families. There were many groups like this, but she realized just how hard it was to find one in her area and secure a spot for her kids.

Raul had been looking to transition as well. He was in higher education and needed to move to a different university. The previous year had been a string of disappointments: making it to the final round of job candidates only to come in second over and over again. Together they were vocationally frustrated and discouraged. They quickly realized they couldn't rely on each other in the same way because they were both in a tailspin. So they decided to invite a mentor of theirs into the conversation.

They got a sitter and found some time to talk through the scenario with their mentor. Lindsey had already done some homework on her childcare center idea. She had researched the training and the costs if she were to start the center out of their home. She wasn't 100 percent sure she was supposed to step away from teaching to start this venture. Through the conversation, they realized she was more sure that she wanted to try than either of them had acknowledged. What they had been waiting on was Raul's job. They had both figured the decision about Lindsey's job would come after Raul's job transition.

This conversation helped them realize that the question wasn't if Lindsey should launch her childcare center but when. The question they were really asking was "Should we take this risk as a family and support Lindsey's vision to start a childcare center even though Raul is still in a job search?" Their mentor encouraged them to step into a couple of different experiments. First, both of them would reach out to other families to see who, among those they already knew, would be willing to enroll in the childcare center. Having committed, paying clients upfront would help mitigate the risk. They made a list and a deadline for those conversations.

They designed the second experiment following the "10-10-10 rule" invented by business writer Suzy Welch.[3] This rule helps you imagine how you'll feel about your decision at different times in the future. Here are the steps they took:

Step 1: They found a time to get away, just the two of them. They planned to spend a day relaxing and resting. The next day, they would start their process.

Step 2: They both brought separate journals, headed to the lake nearby, and sat down to reflect and write. They agreed in advance that Lindsey was more likely to write in her journal bullet by bullet, while Raul was more of a narrative thinker and would need more time to write. They both agreed they wanted to take this time journaling in a posture of prayer, asking God's Spirit to reveal anything that could help them in their next steps.

Step 3: They wrote down two statements in the form of decisions they could hypothetically make. First, they would go ahead and start to launch the childcare center out of their home in the next six months so they could open in September. Second, they would wait to make a move until Raul found a new job.

Step 4: They put both decision statements through the 10-10-10 process, journaling their answers to these questions and trying to imagine what it would be like if this were a final decision:

1. How would I feel about this decision ten minutes from now?
2. How would I feel about this decision ten months from now?
3. How would I feel about this decision ten years from now?

Step 5: Finally, they walked back to their cabin, made dinner, and compared their notes.

Of course, this experiment didn't have to result in a decision. However, by the end of the dinner, they decided that they would choose to wait until Raul got a different job. Through the process, they both realized they were more open to moving to another city if there was a job there that was a good fit for Raul. As much as they loved their community, they had some good friends in a few other cities, and both of them had sensed God reminding them to pay attention to their relationships in this process. They ended up making a whole other decision that weekend: they would expand Raul's job search to universities in two other cities where they had family and friends.

Case Study 2

Yolanda had been living in the Midwest for most of her life. Like many midwesterners, she daydreamed about living in California and not having to deal with the freezing winters she had endured for so many years. She never expected this daydream to become an actual option, but a headhunter asked Yolanda to apply for a position at a company just outside San Francisco. She figured there was no harm in going through the interview process. After all, that's how she got her current position. The process went quickly; they even flew her out for a few days. She had a job offer and an invitation to move if she could do so within a couple of months.

While the daydreams had been fun, deciding to make this move felt way more significant than she could have imagined. She needed to design an experiment—and fast, because she only had a few weeks before they would need an answer. She asked a few friends she trusted to come over and talk through the decision with her. She shared the opportunity with the others and asked them to try to put their personal relationships with her aside as much as possible. But she also told them she did want her relationships here to be a factor in this decision. She paid attention to her friends' questions and reactions as part of her listening process. One friend asked, "How sure would you need to be in order to say yes to this job? I mean, there is no such thing as 100 percent, so which percentage are you shooting for realistically in the next two weeks?"

This question led Yolanda to the experiment she designed. She's a pretty measured and cautious person, so she said she needed to be 80 percent sure before saying yes to the move. Then she outlined these steps:

Step 1: She found a mason jar and ordered one hundred marbles online for a few bucks. Each marble represented 1 percent of her assurance that this was the right decision.

Step 2: She counted out twenty of the marbles and set them aside in a drawer—these represented the 20 percent that would add up to complete certainty. Putting them in the drawer helped her give up certainty as a reality.

Step 3: After talking to her friends, she felt she was about 55 percent sure about saying yes to the job. Her friends were more supportive than she had imagined because they could tell that this could be a great opportunity for her. So she placed fifty-five marbles into the jar.

Step 4: She placed a bowl next to the jar and put the twenty-five additional marbles in the bowl.

Step 5: Over the next two weeks, she had many conversations with friends and family, spent time in prayer, and worked out the numbers, realizing just how much higher the cost of living was in California. After each day, she reflected on the work she'd done and either added marbles to the jar or took some out and put them in the bowl.

Step 6: She gave herself a deadline of two weeks and told a friend she would make the decision that day.

After the two weeks were over, she realized just how much she was wavering back and forth in this decision. Her parents had a lot of questions she didn't know the answers to, which caused her trepidation, so she removed some marbles. She connected online with some of the folks who would be her new team members, and that went so well that she added back a handful of marbles! When she realized that the cost of living meant she was really only getting a small financial promotion, she took some marbles out. When she negotiated a higher salary and realized she could afford more plane tickets and a slightly larger apartment for visitors, she added some marbles. By decision day, she had seventy-six marbles in the jar, and she spent time in prayer and journaling that afternoon. During that time, she felt like Jesus invited her to trust him not just with the 20 percent of uncertainty but with that additional 4 percent as well. She called her friend and blurted out, "I'm making the move!"

Check out the Decision-Making Toolbox for tools to help you in designing your vocational experiments as well as making other decisions.

12

RELATIONAL EXPERIMENTS

Experiments about relating with family, friends, and partners.

We were sitting on the lawn outside of the seminary having lunch, as a group of us had started to do regularly. We were all women in grad school training to be pastors, and that made us a rare species. "These conversations have become one of the best parts of my week!" one of the women exclaimed, and we all agreed. We had been talking about how our experiences as women in the church had formed us and the ways we saw theology differently through not only our stories but those whose cultures and backgrounds were different from ours. We talked about what it could mean for us to truly step into our gifting and leadership even though most of us had experiences of our voices being stifled.

There are times in life when you realize you are experiencing something special, and I felt this was one of those moments. Perhaps you have felt this way before, when you are talking to someone or are around a group of people who make you feel understood and seen. If you haven't had that experience, I truly hope that you do, and perhaps this chapter can guide you toward finding relationships like these again, or for the first time.

What happened next was critical, though at the time I didn't realize to what extent. I invited the women to come over to my house to continue the conversation. We ended up designing an experiment, though I didn't use that language for it back then. We decided to meet every Sunday night for the rest of the academic year and continue the conversations we had been having, but more intentionally. We would take turns sharing our stories as women in leadership and hold the space to listen to each other with a goal of deeper understanding. In short, weeks turned to months, and months into years, and these eight women are still in my life today.

But this didn't happen by accident. Our Sunday-night experiments created a space where God led us to such intentionality in our friendship that we decided to make a lifelong commitment to each other—just like the covenant commitments we see in Scripture. When we made that commitment, there were nine of us, and only two had partners they were married to at the time. As I'm writing this almost eight years later, we are all married, so that makes eighteen adults as well as nine kiddos and counting!

We realized something was special about those lunches, we tried out an experiment while listening to God, and it led us to a twenty-six-person growing family of friendship. This may seem like that moment in a commercial when "Results aren't typical" pops up on the screen. In some ways, this kind of intentionality in friendship is rare, but it doesn't have to be.

RELATIONSHIPS AND FAIRY TALES

The dominant cultures of the Western world tend to have an extreme focus on romantic relationships. This is not news to most of us—we see the focus on sex, romance, and partnership around us almost constantly. Some of us may have experienced a Christian subculture that added some pretty strange twists. I was raised with a hyperglorified view of marriage and a disparaging view of singleness. Yet dating came with a ton of rules and pressure, and sexuality with a heaping dose of shame. While there is wisdom in having conversations with young Jesus followers about God's heart for them when it comes to sexuality and romantic relationships, entire books could be—and have been—written on the problems that have come from the so-called purity culture I was steeped in.

This is not one of those books. However, it is worth acknowledging that our cultural experiences in the realm of relationships deeply shape our approach. So stop now and think about what relationships have meant to you in your life. Not merely romantic relationships—though for many of us, that is our default when we think of the word. Think about what and who shaped you in this area as a kid, a teenager, a young adult. What experiences have you had in adulthood that impact your posture as we broach the topic?

While everyone's experience is different, throughout this chapter I want to address some of the barriers created by common cultural experiences. In my opinion, the hyperfocus on romantic relationships above all other types is a significant barrier to healthy relationships generally. We see this hyperfocus dominate the space from pop culture, to church life, to happy hour, to family reunions. Additionally, we tend to focus not on the reality of a relationship but rather on a fairy tale version where love can overcome everything. The truth is, it can't! If you have trauma, relational wounds, unhealthy family patterns, a history of substance abuse, poor conflict resolution skills, or even just a different communication style than your partner, then you will need to do some relational and emotional work. It's expected that all relationships will need support from friends, a coach, or a therapist, and we all need a whole lot of Jesus. For the record, I've never seen a relationship that didn't check a couple of boxes from that list of relationship stressors.

Writer Shauna Niequist once said, "You are significant even without a significant other."[1] You can see how hard that is to believe given the world's standards for most of us. As a teenager, I was encouraged to pray for my future spouse, to write out lists of what traits I valued in a spouse, and to be on the lookout at all times for that mythical person. While I think prayer can always be helpful, you can see how this encouragement and way of thinking about a future partner can lead to unrealistic expectations. And by focusing on something in the future and incessantly looking around for this mate, you can potentially miss most of what is actually happening right in front of you. What most people need, whether they have a partner or not, are really good friends. People who are loyal and patient but also willing to challenge you. People who will accept you no matter what but also love you too much to accept anything less than growth in your life.

But growing up, no one ever encouraged me to write down what I was looking for in a friend. Or to fast and pray for God to bring people into my life who would surround me in friendship. Given that the culture I grew up in was very influenced by the Bible, it really is fascinating how often they focused on romantic relationships compared to the many other important relationships in our lives. A scan through the New Testament, for instance, leads to many more references to relationships between people of different cultures and social statuses as relationships God calls us to pursue. If there is a hyperfocus on relationships in Scripture, it is on loving one's neighbor. And many passages suggest we need to invest significant time in learning how to love each other like we are all a family even when we are not related by blood or marriage.

The apostle Paul wrote thirteen letters to his friends in various churches in the ancient Near East, and in them, he constantly told them to regard each other as brothers and sisters and to treat younger folks as daughters and sons. He referred to himself as one who loves those he writes to as a father. The Bible is basically a book about relationships—with God and each other. While Scripture mentions spouses throughout, marriage relationships certainly aren't the main focus over all other aspects of what it means to be people created for relationships. So as we continue to discuss the realm of relational experiments, let's try to expand our perspective on how much God values the many relationships in our lives.

In today's world, many of us don't live near our families of origin. Thus sociologists are beginning to study a new type of emerging family called the *framily*—or friends who are like family—that has become a main support system for young adults. Some people have probably heard the word *friendsgiving*, referring to a thanksgiving meal shared between friends, whether or not they have a traditional family meal to attend. TV shows like *Friends*, *Living Single*, and *How I Met Your Mother* are cultural symbols of the rise of the "framily" experience.

Sociologist Rose Coser points out some drawbacks to this kind of emerging community.[2] Strong ties usually form most readily between those who are similar. Homogeneity allows for relationships to form more quickly. While homogeneity can bring mutual understanding—as it did with my friends who are women in ministry—it also keeps us from forming deep relationships with those who are different from us and can create an ingrown cluster of relationships. "Weak ties"—those whom we are connected to, but not as intimately—take us beyond the cluster, helping us network for new jobs or introducing us to a future spouse. When we think about relationships in our lives, it makes sense that we think of the most intimate first, like partners and friends, but it's important to keep the wider community in mind as well.

UNLOCKED DOORS

I've heard the colloquial phrase "God opened a door" or "when God closes a door, God opens a window" and other variations of the same sentiment. While the door and window metaphors may be helpful, to me they are also incomplete. Let's consider this metaphor in regards to relationships—for instance, those with potential friends, spouses, and employers. My experience suggests that God sometimes unlocks doors, but we must choose to open them. I've also experienced seasons when I've needed to keep coming back to a door to see if it's been unlocked; sometimes what was locked for a while may be unlocked later. And God is not the only one metaphorically locking and unlocking or opening and closing doors. Other humans are always involved in the opportunities we each have in life. I also believe that God's enemy has forces of evil in the world that sometimes hold doors shut, and we are meant to break those doors down or pick the lock.

Generally speaking, in the area of relationships, I think many of us tend to default to a more passive approach. I have had so many conversations with men and women who long for deeper friendships but think someone else is going to provide these for them. I've spoken with folks who long for a mentor but think they must wait for someone to come to them and select them as a mentee. This is a time when you need to try the doors and see if any are unlocked. Once we leave the pressure-cooker environment of high school and college, it can be much more difficult to initiate deep friendships, but most things worth doing aren't easy. Yes, it can be awkward to ask someone to be a mentor or a guide in your life for a season. They might even say no! But until you make a move, you'll never know what important relationships could develop and deeply impact your life!

TREATING RELATIONSHIPS LIKE YOUR CAREER

The same cultures that hyperfocus on romantic relationships also tend to place a high value on careers. Americans typically use "So . . . what do you do?" as one of their main ice breakers. The answer to that question could be many things—eat, sleep, stream movies, play racquetball—but we all know the correct answer is to share your job. It's no wonder, since most adults spend most of their waking hours at work. I don't think the focus on careers in dominant culture is going to change any time soon. However, when it comes to community and relationships, we could stand to treat these areas of life with the same tenacity and focus.

We discussed vocational experiments at length in chapter 11. Sometimes we feel stuck, but when we look back on how we got to where we are now in our career and think about where we want to go, some paths are pretty obvious. For instance, you can begin to actively search for a different job. Or you can seek education or training for a new career or to further your career. Networking is important so that you can move beyond your inner circle to draw on your weak ties. It's not always easy or simple to take these steps, but nevertheless, they do offer a clear path forward—at least clearer than most relationships seem to be! What if we tried to think about community, dating, or searching for a mentor in similar ways?

I enjoyed the single life for all of my twenties. But eventually, I felt like it was time to be intentional about dating. I realized that I didn't need a spouse, but I am so companion oriented that I really do feel wired to have a life partner. At first I felt stuck. When I went over the advice often given to me about romantic relationships, it seemed pretty crappy: "They will come when you aren't looking for them." That is a strange one for someone who was literally not looking for a spouse for a better part of a decade and now was looking. Or how about "God has someone in mind for you, but you need to be patient"? If you change that to "God has a job in mind for you, but you just need to be patient," it doesn't make sense, right? If you want a job, you ask your friends and connections if they know of any openings, you apply for a job, you take action, and you ask questions to see if it's a good fit. I personally don't believe that God is going to drop a healthy life partner into your lap any more than God is going to do that with a job or a home or any other aspect of life.

So I approached dating like I would a job search, and I decided to try two experiments. The first was one that many have participated in: the grand experiment of online dating. I'll just say, it seemed fun at first, but it didn't take long before it just felt hard. I told one of my mentors that I wanted to quit, and she asked me, "Do you feel like God is inviting you to actively pursue a relationship right now?"

"I think so," I replied sheepishly.

"Well, figure out if this is what you are being called to pursue right now, because if it is, then you need to treat it like a spiritual discipline," she told me. Whoa! With this perspective, I would need to approach dating like a vocational and spiritual experiment, and in many ways it was. I was going to be someone's wife, which is an aspect of vocation. And now that I have been married for a few years, I can most definitely say it is work!

While online dating has become common, my second experiment was more unconventional. I asked some of my friends and some of my "weak ties" if they were up for a challenge. I told them that anyone who introduced me to my future spouse would be rewarded with a round-trip vacation with me to anywhere in the United States! They were pretty surprised that I offered an actual reward (and I clarified that Hawaii was probably out of my budget), but it worked! No, it didn't work in finding my actual husband—that was achieved through the online app experiment. But it worked because I got set up on some dates with some nice guys and learned more about what I was looking for in a partner. It's kind of like learning what jobs you may actually want by asking questions in an interview even if you don't take that job. After the heartbreak from the breakup I described in part 1, it was tempting to give up on my experiments and stop moving forward. I did take a break after that relationship ended and got some therapy, but then I got back on the horse because that's what I felt God was inviting me into. It was in round four or five of the online experiment that I met my husband, JD, and I'm so glad I didn't give up.

FRIENDSHIP DTR

When I was in college, we figured out ways to communicate in shorthand, sometimes using an acronym or two, like ASAP or RSVP. But we hadn't seen anything yet because that was before the rise of the text message. My fifteen-year-old mentee is always texting me with letters that mean whole sentences, and I often have to google what they mean or have her teach me. Back in what she would call "the olden days," we had the acronym *DTR*, which stood for "define the relationship." This was a conversation you had with someone you were romantically interested in to see what stage the relationship was in. Were you dating? Just friends? Committed? Exclusive? This kind of conversation is intimidating but incredibly helpful when there is ambiguity in the romance department, but I think it can be helpful for other relationships as well.

When you are hoping that a friend you are getting to know will become someone you can trust with struggles you are having with your faith, talking directly about it might be a good idea. If you are getting to know a coworker and think you could be friends beyond the office, consider sharing that hope with them and suggest a happy hour. I know it can seem awkward, but sometimes it's the best way to move forward. If you long for a deeper and more intimate community, no one will do that *for* you, but there are people who will do that *with* you. But you will need to ask.

In terms of relationship experiments, we will all be coming from different places. You must start by thinking about what has shaped you in this area. What have you come to believe about relationships, friendships, and yourself? If you have lies in your mind and heart like "No one wants to spend time with me" or if you hear yourself say, "I'm unlovable" or "I'm undesirable," then you need to pause and pursue the truth. If you realize you have overprioritized the hope for a romantic partner and haven't grown a trustworthy community in your life, I would strongly suggest starting with friendship. I have seen many marriages and families up close, and those that don't have a community to support them always struggle and sometimes fail. No matter what the next step is for you, when you invest in your relationships, you will always get a great return on your relational investment!

CASE STUDIES

Case Study 1

After Tasha and Andrew got married, Tasha was struggling to get to know her new mother-in-law, Adaku. Part of the problem was that Tasha is from a Scandinavian culture and background, and Andrew's family is Nigerian. Andrew was part of the first generation of his family born in the United States after his parents emigrated from Nigeria in the 1970s. On top of these cultural differences, Tasha had also lost her mom to cancer right after the wedding, and that loss was a strain on her as well as Adaku. There was tension between them, and Tasha felt like Adaku had expectations that Tasha could never live up to. Tasha and Andrew had been working on processing the cultural differences, and that had helped them both in relating to each other's families, but Tasha knew something needed to shift specifically between her and her mother-in-law.

They had plans to visit his family in Indianapolis for a long weekend, so she realized this could be an opportunity. She designed a short experiment to see if any progress could be made:

Step 1: She shared with Andrew that she was going to make a specific effort with Adaku that weekend. He was a little nervous because there had been so much tension, but he agreed something needed to happen. She asked him if he could help arrange some time for Tasha and Adaku to spend together, just the two of them, while they were visiting.

Step 2: During the entire visit as well as their time alone together, Tasha prayed that God would lead her each minute as to when to speak, when to listen, and even what to say.

Step 3: She paid close attention to her feelings and shared them with Andrew each night so she was able to stay present. He committed to pray for her as well.

Step 4: This short experiment would end when they traveled home, but Tasha prayed that she would learn from this experiment and that she would be able to apply what she had learned to future interactions.

What happened was beyond what Tasha had imagined. She followed the steps, and during some time alone with Adaku in the kitchen, she tried her best to listen to God. She realized she had always tried to fill the space between them with words because she was feeling so anxious around Adaku. She had a sense that God wanted her to stay quiet and listen; in that space, Adaku invited her to help with the food she was making. This was the first time she had invited Tasha to participate. In the past, she had always said no when Tasha had asked if she needed help.

Adaku began to explain the process of cooking jollof, a rice dish that's an important staple in any Nigerian household. Tasha silently listened while chopping the tomatoes and trying to eye how much of each spice would be used. (Adaku didn't use any measuring utensils.) And then, almost as though someone were whispering in her ear, she felt God say to her, "Ask her how to say *mom*." Because she had committed to following anything she thought she heard from God, she waited until there was silence and said, "Adaku, how do you say the word for *mom* or *mother* in Igbo?" Igbo was the language of their Nigerian tribe. Andrew always used the English word *mom* when referring to Adaku, so Tasha realized she had no idea.

"It is pronounced 'nne,' kind of like 'knee' in English, but slightly different," Adaku responded, pronouncing it again for Tasha.

Immediately Tasha felt tears coming to her eyes, and she knew right away what she needed to do: "Is it OK if I call you by this term? After losing my mom, it's hard for me to refer to anyone else this way, but I am so thankful to have a chance to have another mom in my life." Now it was Adaku's turn to tear up. She shared how she thought perhaps Tasha was not happy to be her daughter-in-law, and that was why she hadn't called her "mom." Now, years later, Tasha looks back on this weekend as a turning point in her relationship with Adaku but also in processing the loss of her own mom.

Case Study 2

José and Tina moved to Milwaukee from Chicago because of a job transfer for José. They were excited to live in a smaller city, but they didn't realize that leaving their community in Chicago would be so hard. They had friends with whom they had connected soon after they started going to their church in Chicago. To make it even more difficult, they had just had their first child. They quickly found a church in Milwaukee they loved and that was encouraging, but after a year, they still hadn't made any connections with others. They knew having a little one they needed to race home for a nap wasn't helping.

The church was good at helping folks find small groups, but the group time frames conflicted with Tina's new job. Because they were so young, they got lumped in with other young professionals who didn't yet have kids, and this made it hard to connect at a time that was reasonable with a two-year-old. When they talked with the community life pastor, she suggested they reach out to another couple who lived a few blocks from them. They connected with this couple right away because they also had a toddler, so they had them over for dinner. They realized between chasing the kids around that both families were longing for intergenerational relationships, since they were now raising little ones with no grandparents or aunts and uncles nearby.

Together the two couples decided to do an experiment. Their church had connected people in many different ways: based on interest in the same book study, or what life stage they were in, or even what night of the week they happened to be free. But they didn't have any formal way to connect people geographically. So they outlined their steps:

Step 1: From talking with the pastor, they realized they could use their church database to find the addresses of others in their community. They looked up the families and individuals who lived closest to them.

Step 2: They crafted an email to these eight families, sharing who they were and inviting them to a gathering at a local park within walking distance.

Step 3: They brought some lawn games and toys for the kids and invited people to bring their favorite snack food.

Step 4: When it seemed like most people had arrived, they had everyone go around and introduce themselves and where they lived. They knew from the list that the group had folks from all different generations, since they were connecting by geography rather than life stage.

Step 5: They briefly shared what they felt God had put in their hearts for intergenerational relationships and said they wanted to host these park nights every other week all summer to form intentional relationships with their neighbors from church. They also shared that they would love for the park nights to be spaces where other neighbors, not just those who went to their church, could be invited.

Step 6: They promised to follow up with an email later that week, and anyone who didn't want to be on further emails could opt out, with no judgment whatsoever: "We just ask that you pray about it and be honest if this really isn't something you have time for. We don't want to fill up anyone's inbox!"

After one summer of this experiment, some wonderful relationships were built. However, it was not the ones that they would have expected at first. There was a couple in their forties with no kids who actually seemed super-reserved and introverted, but Tina and José's little girl really took to them, and so a local surrogate aunt and uncle were found! A few single women in their twenties and one widower in his eighties formed a little extended family that was an answer to each of their prayers. Tina and José also connected with many neighbors who were not Christians who began to be a part of their wider neighborhood group. They had many opportunities to share meals and support and be supported by their neighbors. After the community life pastor asked them to share about the experience in a video for the worship service, the next summer a couple of other neighborhoods at their church gave it a try!

Check out the Decision-Making Toolbox in the appendix for tools to help you in designing your relational experiments as well as making other decisions.

PART 3

MOVE INTO YOUR FUTURE

Never be afraid to trust an unknown future to a known God.

—Corrie ten Boom

13

OTHER EXPERIMENTS AS NEEDED

*What is the best experiment to perform
when I don't know what to do?*

*What if the experimentation is overwhelming
due to a lack of time and energy?*

My niece, Mabel, has the energy and charisma at three years old that most of us would hope to have in our whole lifetime. Like many other young girls and boys today, she can sing every song from the animated movies *Frozen* and *Frozen 2*. Those of you who are familiar with the first movie are no doubt very aware of the ballad "Let It Go," which is belted out by the main character, Elsa. The problem with so many kiddos giving their own renditions of the song is that the range is superwide and hard to sing. Even the voice actor, Idina Menzel, can't hit the notes some days!

We all thought this second movie wouldn't be able to match the extreme popularity of the first or provide another song to rival the earworm "Let It Go." But they did it again with a song called "Into the Unknown," sung again by Idina as Elsa. The main character is realizing just how uncertain her future truly is and how much she doesn't know about life, her family, and even herself. This song exploded as the world barreled into 2020 and all that came with it. This isn't the first time I've seen Disney Animation as prophetic; I'm still uncomfortable with how much the lockdown due to the coronavirus pandemic seemed like a scene right out of the 2008 Disney Pixar film *WALL-E*. If you haven't seen it, consider this your trigger warning.

"Into the Unknown"—this is the reality of all our lives even if we don't realize it. We experience the most anxiety on those days when we are aware of just how little control we truly have in life. I watch Mabel twirl around singing the lyrics: "There's a thousand reasons I should go about my day and ignore your whispers, which I wish would go away." She has no idea what it will be like someday to be a grown-up and realize the pressure of the decisions facing her. How do we move into the future with confidence when we truly are moving into the unknown?

AN ADVENTURE INVITATION OF LOVE

In *Frozen 2*, Queen Elsa hears a voice calling to her that she is trying to ignore, and I realize I often respond to God's voice in my life that way. She tries to listen, but it's unclear what the voice is trying to say, and fear rises up in her. She's feeling lost and confused, and this voice is making it worse because her attempts to ignore it are failing: "You're not a voice; you're just a ringing in my ear." I understand wanting to just settle into life, to ignore the way that God beckons us to trust the Spirit and follow him into the unknown future. Elsa finally gives in, admitting that she feels a growing longing to step into this adventure. The ballad concludes with her willingness to go for it, asking this voice how she is supposed to follow it into the unknown.

God's invitation to follow the Spirit, even though we don't know where we might be led, is motivated by God's deep love for us. No matter how scary it may be to take a risk and experiment, this adventure is exactly what Jesus means when he says he came so that we could have life to the full.[1] God loves you too much to let you stay in your comfort zone, because that truly is not the way to experience God's heart for you.

That may be a great question to ask in your listening process: "God, what is your heart for me? What is it that you want for me?" We often ask, "God, what is it you want from me?" perhaps as an accusation or out of desperation. What God wants from you is your heart and your life. When we give our lives to God, we can experience what God wants *for* us, not *from* us. So I encourage you to ask, "God, what do you want *for* me?"

Imagine what you'd hear back from God if you were to ask that question and really lean in and listen. I don't think you'd ever hear God reply, "My heart for you is that you should settle for average so that you don't ever put yourself at risk." Life following God will never be boring. Sure, you will have seasons where you will experience more of the mundane, but consistent boredom and a life following God's Spirit are not compatible.

EVERY DAY IS AN EXPERIMENT

In *Frozen 2*, Elsa's sister, Anna, also sings a song, "The Next Right Thing," in which she too is facing the unknown. She realizes that she can't see the full picture of what will happen, so all she can do is take it one step at a time. My friend Emily P. Freeman wrote a book by the same name as the song. I hope the movie's popularity somehow increased the popularity of her book, because it's excellent. She points out that this phrase has been made popular given that it is found in the *Big Book of Alcoholics Anonymous*. Emily suggests that we don't have to be addicted to substances to realize that we may be addicted to clarity and certainty. I can think of a few other "addictions" we may face: addictions to control, safety, and comfort. She writes, "If you are facing something and you don't know where to start, maybe doing the next right thing will be a welcome beginning."[2]

In the first part of this book, we talked about another addiction: the addiction to being right or correct. So with all due respect to Alcoholics Anonymous, to Emily, and to the many others who have hung onto this important phrase, my slight edit would be "Do the next *best* thing." Try to take the pressure off yourself a little and recognize that you can never be certain what is *right*, but there are often a few good next options. All you can do is the *best* you can.

The story of the people of God in the wilderness from Exodus is a great example of just doing the best we can to follow God every day. Every day, they woke up and their job was to look for the pillar of fire, which they believed was a manifestation of God's Spirit. When they woke up and saw the pillar had not moved, they stayed put, and if it moved, they packed up camp and moved themselves. While the number of people who left Egypt is debated[3] by scholars, we know hundreds of families left Egypt and made camp under the pillar of the fire of God's presence, so getting up to go was not an easy or simple thing to do.

When we think about what the fire represented, we can see why it was worth it. It should inspire all of us to try to make our camp beneath the presence of God each day. I'm sure there were many days where that didn't feel all that interesting or adventurous, but other days, it must have been amazing to look up into the night sky and see a representation of the God of the Universe. Isn't that just like our lives? Many days feel like drudgery, and we just do what we need to do to make it to the weekend or whatever else we have in front of us. But other days, we look out at a beautiful sunset or into the eyes of one of our kids, and we experience a sense of awe that reminds us we are camped under the presence of God!

There are those days that feel like they are dripping with meaning and purpose—where we are engaging in something and we think, "I feel made for this." We were made to join God's work in the world. God created each of us with specific wiring and passions in order to join that work in our own ways. So if the Spirit of God is shifting, don't be afraid to pick up camp and make a move.

LITTLE EXPERIMENTS THAT CAN TEACH US A LOT

God cares about the little decisions we make each day. I'm not suggesting we must fast and pray before deciding to go on a walk versus a bike ride. What I am suggesting is that God cares so much for you, and God is deeply interested in the details of your life. We so easily assume God only really cares about the big decisions regarding vocation and relationships. But God also cares about our calendars and our to-do lists. God cares about our energy levels and our time management. Now, I'm not saying God wants to control our Google Calendars, but what if we were to let God's Spirit into how we use our time and energy?

One summer I was living with my friend Christian Ann, and we realized the upcoming summer months weren't really all that full and planned. We were both in school, so we had a lighter load in the summer when it came to work and education. The temptation is sometimes to fill up summer break with other activities—causing the *break* part to get lost in the fray. We had no money, so we decided to design some experiments that had to do with everyday life to see what we might learn and also to keep a long, hot summer interesting.

We went a week without spending any money. We ran out of gas by Thursday, ended up eating deep into the cans in the pantry, and had to beg for a few items, like stamps, vegetable oil, and eggs. One week we didn't use any lights, and at night we only used candles, which was the strangest in the bathroom. The most expensive week was when we made or ate every meal intentionally from a different culture. I wish we could have kept that experiment going every week—it tasted so good!

At the end of that summer, we had learned a lot about ourselves. We both had a deep sense that God was present even in those experiments that may have seemed silly or small. If you are finding yourself in a rut, reach out to a friend and create some experiments! It could be just the thing to mix things up for you. If you have kids, I highly recommend getting them involved in experimenting at a young age so that as they grow up, they will be more prepared to step into the unknown and not just scream the song at the top of their lungs!

WHAT EXPERIMENT SHOULD I TRY WHEN I DON'T KNOW WHAT TO DO?

I love thinking about the game Jenga when it comes to figuring out in what area of life to design an experiment. The idea of Jenga is to stack fifty-four little blocks up in a tower and try to remove one brick at a time without knocking over the stack. Our lives feel this way sometimes, as if every big decision we make could topple our life over. In Jenga and in life, there are a variety of possible approaches. Some folks don't have much fear of the bricks falling, so they go for it, and often the bricks do fall. I've seen people approach decisions not recognizing how much was riding on them, and friends have had to help them pick up the pieces.

Then others carefully observe and try to think which brick may be the best next step for them just through observation. Then when it's their turn, they are nervous and even find their hands shaking a little. Before they can really decide which brick to take, their shaking hands cause the tower to topple. Or these same folks cause their friends frustration because they take so long at their turn and freeze up with fear.

Those who are masters at the game quickly and ever so lightly tap the bricks right in their center, looking for the loose one. Then they tap just a bit harder, and a bit more, and soon that brick slides right out without any chance of toppling the tower. When it comes to life, what would "tapping the bricks" look like for you? When you need to perform an experiment but you don't know what to do, how might you figure out what may be a loose brick for you? I think of these as lower-risk experiments that won't nec-essarily lead to long-term, permanent decisions. Tapping a brick could be as simple as trying out a new hobby. When we hit big age milestones like thirty or forty, it may be time to try something new. If you are an empty-nester or retiree, this is a great time to experiment with a hobby or a new purpose experiment that could inject some energy into your next season.

I picked up stand-up paddleboarding in my midthirties, and I found out, much to my relief, that it was much easier than it looks. "Tapping the brick" looked like renting a board, wearing a life jacket, and giving it a try with a friend. Now I'm all in with my own boards, the right rack on my car—the whole nine! To prove that God even cares about our hobbies, I have found that being on a paddleboard in the center of a large body of water is one of the most consistent ways I experience God's presence these days. Nothing else I do regularly gives me that same feeling.

The illustration can be applied to the specific areas of life we discussed in part 2. When you feel like you may need to make a move when it comes to relationships, tapping a brick may look like signing up for a meetup where you could find a new hobby and some new friends. Or asking a friend what their experience with online dating has been like before you jump into the deep end. When it comes to vocation, tapping a brick may look like reaching out for a coffee with a "weak tie" relation in a field that intrigues you. You can apply the idea of tapping the Jenga brick to any area of life where you need to see what move you might be ready to make. This is also a great approach to talk through with a spouse or business partner. Talking through which bricks you will metaphorically tap can help people get on the same page when they are at a crossroads.

TIME AND ENERGY EXPERIMENTS

I have coached hundreds of people in making decisions and trying to follow God's direction in their lives. I often say, "The only failed experiment is the one you don't do." You may not have the outcome you are hoping for when it comes to your experiment, but that is not the same as a failed experiment. Each experiment is an opportunity to learn and leads us to the next best step forward. So what is it that keeps people from actually doing the experiments they set out to explore? Sometimes their steps weren't very clear, and that holds them back. Other times they realize they aren't asking the question they thought they were originally, so they throw out their experiment to change gears and try a different one.

More than anything, we fail to experiment because we are so busy, stressed, and overwhelmed that we just don't do it. Sometimes when my coaching clients and I are planning an experiment, they can get pumped up and excited to give it a try. But that isn't enough when the busyness of life takes over. When this is the case, I suggest people take a step back and do some experiments regarding their time and energy. What could you try that may help you get some time and energy back? If your brain jumped to "dropping out of school" or "giving my kids to someone else to raise for a while," then may I suggest you *really* need to experiment in this area because you are *wiped*!

A great way to begin is to think of all aspects of your life as the cumulative "capital." My friend Mike Breen was the first one to reframe this concept for me, because I had often thought of capital as only financial and material.[4] He suggests that there are five forms of capital in life, and he puts them in order of importance. First is *spiritual capital*, which has a currency of wisdom and spiritual power. The next most important capital we have is our *relational capital*, measured in depth of trust and quality of our relationships with family, friends, and colleagues. In the middle of the list is *physical capital*, which is our time and energy and our capacity to use them well. Then there is *intellectual capital*, which has a currency made of thoughts, ideas, knowledge, and creativity. Finally, we have what we all typically think of when it comes to capital and equity, and that is *financial capital*, measured in dollars and cents (or whatever currency your economic system uses).

While spiritual capital is the most important, it is also the most difficult to measure. Mike suggests it is also the most difficult to acquire. That means financial capital would be the easiest to acquire. We all know that earning money isn't exactly *easy*, but upon further reflection, you may see what he means. You can't buy the other forms of capital.

We can design experiments that will leverage our different kinds of capital together, and in so doing, we can create opportunities that we wouldn't have if we didn't see how these forms of capital interacted. This is not a "money can buy happiness" theory. But for instance, money can buy the time of someone who can clean your house every other week, and that means you will have more time and energy for your kids. That could be an experiment right there! It may mean cutting back costs in another area, but it could be worth it.

We can leverage our relational capital by realizing that there are perhaps folks younger than us who would love a chance to "pick our brains" on a subject we know more about. Many people have opened up some time and energy to invest in these relationships and found the benefits are much more reciprocal. For example, you might count on these young folks to pick up your kids when you are running late or take you to the airport and thus save you money. It may take a new type of thinking to consider these "leveraging your capital" experiments, but I am only able to accomplish things in my life with a lot of help, and leveraging capital helps me get there! For instance, paying a spiritual director for twelve years has helped me grow my spiritual capital significantly, but it costs financial capital as well as time when I think I could be doing something more productive. However, that investment has been worth every penny and every minute.

FOLLOW THE FRUIT

When it comes to the crisis of exhaustion, stress, and busyness, I encourage you to think about pruning. This concept is found most prominently in John 15, where Jesus uses the illustration of a vine and its fruit. Of course, the concept of pruning is found anywhere plants are found! The basic idea is that plants will grow and be healthy only if we cut them back to create space so they can grow new branches. Plants can put more energy into those branches after the weakest are removed. We are like this as well. When we have too many branches growing in our lives, we end up not having enough energy for all of them to thrive and "bear fruit."

In John 15, Jesus points out that even some branches that do have fruit on them need to be cut, because the fruit from those branches won't produce abundant, lasting fruit. To grow lasting and abundant fruit in your life, you have to let go of the dead branches as well as those whose fruit is not great. This is such a hard thing to do, especially when we may be cutting out something that still has some juice left in it!

For example, you may be in a book club right now that you have participated in for a few years. You've enjoyed the people in the group, but right now, you just don't have as much time to read the books and give up one night a month to gather and discuss. You haven't dropped out of the club because technically you can cram it into your schedule, and you like the people and don't want to disappoint them. You realize this is an example of the branch that still bears fruit, but not much. You also realize that just because you have the time in your calendar doesn't mean you have the energy. An experiment may be to let the others know how you are feeling and that you are skipping the next book to see if you feel differently about your time and energy.

Putting something on pause, but with intention, can be a great experiment!

When it comes to the little experiments in life, as well as the more significant, you can learn a profound lesson from this vine-and-branches metaphor. When you see fruit in your life—things that look and feel like spiritual and relational capital—it's smart to follow that fruit! That may mean letting go of other things to invest more in the areas where you see growth. When it comes to fruit vines and also our lives, the promise of pruning is growth, and the promise of growth is fruitfulness. Pick some experiments that help you follow the fruit, and you'll be so glad you did. This way, you can live a life that may be full, but not overcome with busyness.

14

DISCERNMENT IN DISRUPTION

*What does it look like to experiment when
everything has suddenly changed?*

On March 13, 2020, I had an awesome weekend planned with my husband to celebrate our anniversary. We had a gift card to a swanky, hipster hotel in downtown Minneapolis with a cocktail bar and a huge hot tub on the roof. When I made that reservation, I had no idea that COVID-19 would be declared a global pandemic that very same week. I couldn't have known that the public school where my church had worshipped since I helped it launch twelve years ago would suspend its lease immediately and indefinitely. I didn't know that my book tour for *Stay Curious* would come to a shrieking halt and that my husband and I, our roommate, and two energetic dogs would be confined to our eight-hundred-square-foot house for months on end.

We didn't see that disruption coming.

While scientists have been warning us for decades that a global pandemic was inevitable, for us as the general public, there is no preparing for something that ominous and elusive. The year 2020 might just be the most disruptive of my life—and perhaps you'd say the same—but if I zoom out a bit and look back on my life, I can think of plenty of other disruptions that have knocked me off my feet. Loss of a loved one, betrayal of a friend, physical illness—I bet you can make your own list. We are often tempted to treat disruptions as interruptions. It's like when the feed cuts out on a video stream—we pause and wonder how long it will take until it's back, but it's usually only a few seconds until the video picks up right where we left off. But a disruption is something that likely won't let us ever return to what was.

Life has more disruptions than interruptions. Most of the time, when something significant happens, there is no "going back to normal." There is what I often call a "new abnormal," followed by a "new normal"—that is, until the next disruption. "Going back to normal" won't be possible post-COVID. The effects of the pandemic will shift and change some things forever. But disruption is not always bad. In the startup world, the term *disruption* has long been used with vigor and excitement. A new company wants to "disrupt the industry" or "upend the status quo" with their new product or service. While I don't want to minimize the pain and suffering that usually accompanies a disruption (and I especially don't want to minimize the devastating loss of life caused by COVID-19), it's important that we also see the benefits that result from almost every disruption. What if disruption, even if its impetus is painful, opens up something new that we desperately need?

DO YOU NOT PERCEIVE IT?

In the seventh century BCE, a man named Isaiah was given the task by God to write down and speak some words for God's people—so he is referred to as Isaiah the Prophet. At that time, the people were exiled in the land of Babylon, where they never expected to be. A series of disruptions had left them living under the oppressive rule of the Babylonian superpower and experiencing a lot of strain and struggle. In Isaiah 43, the prophet speaks God's words to God's people:

> But now, this is what the Lord says—
>> he who created you, Jacob,
>> he who formed you, Israel:
>
> "Do not fear, for I have redeemed you;
>> I have summoned you by name; you are mine.
>
> When you pass through the waters,
>> I will be with you;
> and when you pass through the rivers,
>> they will not sweep over you.
> When you walk through the fire,
>> you will not be burned;
>> the flames will not set you ablaze.
>
> For I am the Lord your God,
>> the Holy One of Israel, your Savior."[1]

These images of passing through rivers and walking through fire are powerful, and I bet that is absolutely how it must have felt to be in their situation. I'm sure you can resonate with this as well. Another image used here—a common one in the Scriptures—is that of a wilderness. Disruption often plops us right into a wilderness experience. It also can wake us up to the fact that we have been in the wilderness for a while without knowing it. Some people had that experience with the pandemic. While it was hard to be home all the time with their spouse or their kids, they realized how much distance had come between them in the prepandemic world. People who lost their jobs were in the wilderness of unemployment but also realized that their job wasn't exactly a mountaintop experience either. Many people began to make career shifts due to the economic crisis. I know many who have been experimenting in this area since the pandemic began.

But here the prophet is assuring the people that God is with them no matter what. They will be in the proverbial river, fire, and wilderness, but God says, "I am the one who made you, I know you, I'm your leader, and I won't leave your side no matter what you face."

Later in the same chapter, Isaiah names the things God had done—how God had rescued them in the past and had been with them through so much. An important part of the disruption process is to stop and remember God's faithfulness to us. No matter what we have been through, we are still here, and God was with us then and is still with us even if it doesn't feel like it right now. Isaiah then gives this interesting message to these struggling people:

"Forget the former things;
    do not dwell on the past.
See, I am doing a new thing!
    Now it springs up; do you not perceive it?
I am making a way in the wilderness
    and streams in the wasteland.

The wild animals honor me,
    the jackals and the owls,
because I provide water in the wilderness
    and streams in the wasteland,

to give drink to my people, my chosen,
    the people I formed for myself
    that they may proclaim my praise."[2]

What a strange turn of phrase! The people are to "forget" the things they see when they look back, and the next line shows us why: if they have their eyes fixed on the past, they won't have their eyes up and ready to perceive what God may be doing in the present. Notice that God doesn't say something like "Don't dwell on the past; instead, look into this crystal ball and see that everything will be fine in the future." No, instead Isaiah says that God is doing something new right now—not in the past, not later on, but now. So when we face disruption, will we have our eyes up to see what is right around us? Or will we be looking back? We may need to use the squinting faith I talked about in chapter 4, but "eyes up" is a mantra in my life whenever I face disruption—even if on a daily basis that just means having my eyes up from my phone, social media, and the barrage of news coverage.

Then God gives the people a clue as to what to look for: the way in the wilderness, the streams in the wasteland, the drink the people need. When a disruption causes you to wake up and see that you are in a wilderness—and perhaps you have been for a while—it's time to look up for the way through. It's time to open your ears and listen for the sound of the streams, just like the trees that move their roots toward the vibrations of the water, listening for the very thing they need the most.

When disruption comes, we can look back and see God's faithfulness, we can look around and see that God is with us, we can look up to see that God is doing a new thing, and we can look for the promise of the refreshing drink God has for us. We should be careful not to make assumptions about what that drink may be. The water of life that God offers us is not always what we would wish for, but it's always what we need. God makes something clear at the end of this passage: that all of this looking and perceiving will lead to praising God. We serve a God who chooses to do a new thing when something difficult or even terrible happens, and that is grace. Most of us will spend our whole lives wondering and searching for why the most difficult things we face have to happen. I don't believe God causes any pain, but it certainly leads me to praise God when I can see that God has used every disruption and hardship in my life to help me grow or lead me to make a move that is positive in the long term.

SPINNING INTO DISILLUSIONMENT

dis·il·lu·sion·ment

> the condition of being disenchanted: the condition of being dissatisfied or defeated in expectation or hope
> also: to free from illusion[3]

Disruption leads to disillusionment nearly every time. Depending on your situation, different aspects of the definition above might resonate. The pandemic freed us from the illusion that modern medicine, our economy, and our social safety nets were enough to protect us from terrible outcomes. Betrayal by someone you trusted might cause "the condition of being disenchanted." Even those who view life through rose-colored glasses and are good at identifying silver linings find themselves disillusioned at times. The question isn't *if* we will experience disillusionment but rather *What will we do with it?*

Imagine a spinning top sitting on a table between us, like those little ones kids can get at the dollar store. With enough practice, a person can get the top to spin for a long time. Eventually, it will come to a stop and fall over, but if it is spun well, you could watch it spin more times than you could possibly count. Daily life often feels like this, with only inertia keeping us going. We move through our daily habits and hobbies, our relationship with God and others, our work and our play.

But if I were to tap that spinning top ever so slightly, it would begin to wobble. That is not a good sign; a wobbling top almost never goes back to spinning with ease. Disruptions in life, big and small, knock our life out of equilibrium, as if our top starts to wobble and our life is spinning out of control.

If we want to get our equilibrium back, we need to metaphorically stop the top from spinning, or slow down and stop long enough to assess what has happened. But many of us worry that if we stop intentionally, it may be hard to get going again. We don't like to further disrupt whatever inertia we had going for us. Or perhaps stopping to attend to some grief or fear sounds scary. We might worry that taking such a pause will cause us to be perceived as weak or vulnerable. But delaying our intentional stop can be a big mistake. Eventually, the top will spin out of control and fall over, but the likelihood of the top spinning out of control and right off of the table is high if we don't choose to stop it intentionally while it is just wobbling.

Disillusionment causes us to get stuck and not make the decision to intentionally stop and get back to spinning again without a dangerous wobble. I see this happen to people all the time. They know things aren't going well in their relationship, it's spinning all wobbly, but one or the other or both don't want to do what it takes to stop, assess the situation, and get the help and tools they need. Another person hits a wall in their faith because they realize a spiritual mentor in their life can't be trusted. This gets their metaphorical top wobbling. Instead of stopping to keep from spinning out of control, they let their experience of faith, their connection to a faith community, and even their personal relationship with God just collapse like a top that spins into a final resting place, motionless.

When we respond passively to disillusionment, we can easily create a pattern that is hard to break when we inevitably face another experience of disillusionment in our lives. Walking out of a friendship you are disillusioned with creates a worn path in your mind and heart that makes it even easier to walk out of a marriage you are disillusioned with. When a job you don't care about goes from fine to toxic and disillusionment causes you to wait until the situation is so bad that you are fired, or you experience deep trauma, how will you break that pattern when you experience some form of disillusionment in a job you care about in the future?

Trust me, indecision is still a decision. When we fail to face reality and stop the top from spinning, we are delaying something difficult and trading it in for something almost unbearable. Many of us learn this lesson the hard way, but it doesn't have to be that way. If we accept that disillusionment is a part of life, then we may recognize it earlier, choose to be brave, and face it head-on instead of waiting to spin out of control.

THE NEW ABNORMAL

When we experience a disruption, we may need some time to grieve what has been lost, and we may need to attend to some trauma. Hopefully, by now you know how much I long for each of us to be emotionally healthy versions of ourselves that take our holistic needs into account. However, at some point, we need to do the hard work of getting going again because God wants to do something new! Jesus says he is making all things new—change and all that comes with it is a part of God's plan. If God is restoring things, then they are constantly shifting and changing. We will explore our relationship with change more in the next chapter. However, when a change comes through a disruption we were not looking for, hoping for, or asking for, we have to choose to accept the new abnormal and then eventually the new normal. That acceptance will give us the opportunity to receive the drink God promises us in the middle of the wasteland. It is the first step in finding our way out of the wilderness.

15

MOVING THROUGH CHANGE

How does experimenting help me cope
with the reality of constant change?

I was sitting with some friends at a Vietnamese restaurant at the end of the block where I used to live. I had only moved a mile away, but something felt strangely sad about going back into that restaurant for the first time after having moved. If you look up the etymology of the word *nostalgic*, you will see it is derived from the Greek words *nostos*, which means "return home," and *algos*, which means "pain." So I was experiencing nostalgia—pain as I returned to what was once my home.

For six years, I had lived on this block, and during that time I had seventeen different roommates. It was a season in my life that I absolutely loved. I had the chance to encourage and mentor the younger women living with me, and in turn I was offered deep friendships from each of them. We had been so intentional about getting to know and love our neighbors, doing our best to follow Jesus's greatest commandments. We threw some amazing block parties, witnessed multiple marriage proposals, and had some heartbreaking experiences as well. It was a time that I will treasure forever.

When we moved, each of us was moving on to great things. I was flipping a new house, dating the guy who became my husband, and besides, I wasn't going too far away. All of this stifled the impact of this huge change I was experiencing. Going back to that Vietnamese restaurant created a pang of "home pain" because I had experienced such significant change in just a few years. I was now married, those seventeen women were literally living all around the world, babies had been born, and so much more. Mostly good things, but somehow it still hurt.

I opened my fortune cookie, which always made me feel a little snarky ever since I heard a public radio show on the dude in New York City who writes the little fortunes as his job. I looked down at the fortune and read it out loud: "When you're finished changing, you're finished." Oh wow, that guy in NYC wasn't a fortune-teller—he was a mind reader! Now, it was just a cookie, but it did shift my perspective from nostalgia to gratitude. Everyone handles change differently, but it is a challenge for all of us in some respect. But if the fortune cookie is right—which they always are—then how can we embrace the way that experimenting can help us move through the change that life brings?

THE TRANSITION TRAIN

Heraclitus, a Greek philosopher, is given credit for the saying "Change is the only constant in life."[1] If you are what I like to call a "change optimist," then perhaps this phrase fills you with anticipation rather than dread. But most people are not change optimists, or even change realists—they are change pessimists. Time and time again, when people are given the option to keep what they have or change to something better, they will choose to avoid the change. Think of all those who resist the chance to update their phone or computer because they don't want the updates to change how things work. The very nature of an update is that it's better—that's the "up" part!

It seems like most people are genuinely afraid of change. But I want to suggest that they don't fear change; they fear loss, and change always means something is lost. We have a deep visceral reaction to loss even when what we are losing wasn't that great in the first place. But it was familiar, and familiarity brings consistency and comfort to our lives. Writer Anatole France wrote in one of his novels, "All changes, even the most longed for, have their melancholy; for what we leave behind us is a part of ourselves."[2]

So how can we move through change? A good first step is to accept that change is constant. I have often thought of change and transition as a train, since I live near several train lines. I can almost always hear the noises from the train yard. Change is as constant in our lives as the trains rolling through my neighborhood. The transition train sometimes moves slowly, and other times you can feel it pick up speed. At times, the train moves so fast you need to hold on for dear life, and other times it rolls slowly enough that you feel every ounce of grief as you watch landscapes slowly fade into the distance. I think of those whose loved ones are in hospice, often for longer than expected. The transition train rolls slowly, and part of you might wish it would come to a stop so that you could have more time or go back to what used to be. Another part of you might wish the train would speed up so that you could get past the gut-wrenching pain of losing someone so slowly.

Other times, the train can feel exciting, the pace is nice, and you are enjoying the scenery along the way. It's almost like a sensory overload experience. It's not until the train slows down a bit that you realize that even a season of positive transitions can be tiring. If we accept that change is constant, then we are less likely to use "times of transition" as an excuse for why we aren't developing healthy rhythms in life. We won't hear ourselves saying things like "There has just been so much transition; I haven't gotten started on that project." Thinking that a season of change will come to a complete stop is one of the most common reasons I have heard people use for why they didn't step into something they were passionate about.

The next step to help us move through change well is to intentionally stop resisting it. We all resist change in different ways. Start to pay attention to your own patterns and notice signs of your resistance to change. It doesn't mean that you must always pursue the next or new thing. It's really more about how those external ways you resist change can help you see where you are *internally* resisting change.

Resisting is like holding tight and clamping down on something you don't want to let go of. When you stop resisting, you can release whatever you are holding on to. That is the process of grieving a loss—you slowly release your grip on what or who is gone. If we become open-handed as we grieve, then we have our hands open to receive. I have found it helps to actually put a hand out in front of you and make a fist that represents what you are holding on to. Then release the grip slowly finger by finger, asking God to help you grieve and let go. You will then have an open hand ready to receive what God has for you. That's a good little practice to remember when you feel yourself resisting the grief that comes with change: "In order to receive what God has for me, I need to let go and grieve."

CHANGE YOUR MINDSET

Thinking of change as a transition train has its limitations as an analogy. Another helpful picture is the idea of a sea of change. While the ocean is massive and represents the unknown, we also know much about it. We know that it is wet. We know that it is salty. The ocean tide will rise and fall like clockwork, and while waves can come in slowly or quickly and range from large to small, they are predictable in many ways as well. Getting good at change is easier when we realize how much is consistent even though change is constant.

Being in the sea of change means we can begin to learn to ride the waves. I am landlocked in Minnesota, but whenever I have the opportunity to travel to the coast, I make a point to take in the sea as much as possible. I have never tried to surf, but I have watched some people try to learn on recent trips to the ocean. It's not pretty at first; they typically crash into the waves and often wind up underwater. But these folks can swim, so they navigate back to shore, get up, and try again. Soon they learn to ride the rhythm of the waves, and then they are ready to take on bigger and stronger waves as they come. We can learn in this same way when it comes to change. We can learn to balance better as we practice riding the smaller waves at first. When we are faced with smaller transitions in life, it can be a good time to reflect on how we process change and what happens in our minds and hearts as we move through the transition. If we can be intentional about growing when we face smaller life changes, it will build our capacity for the larger shifts we will inevitably experience in life. As we continue on our journey, we begin to expect and anticipate some waves to be larger than others and learn how to join the flow of change as it comes in different seasons of our lives.

In many ways, our society is changing faster than it ever has. That means loss is happening at a faster rate as well. The good news is that our capacity to handle change well isn't static; we can grow in our ability to manage the transitions in our lives. We also must learn how to support each other more and more as we experience change at a record-breaking pace. It's much more fun to ride the waves of change together than out on our own. It's also a lot safer to have friends with you when you are surfing, for instance. When it comes to our emotional safety, we need our support system to find wholeness in the midst of the waves.

Experimenting is such a helpful concept when it comes to managing change in our lives. In many ways, it slows down the change process, since deciding to experiment is not the same as making a final decision. Often when we approach change, all we can see is the huge wave coming for us, and then we have no concept of how to safely navigate what is coming at us. Like many things in life, if we stop and think of the steps we want to take to navigate the change, then we will be more likely not to get pummeled and knocked off our feet. As difficult as it may feel when the waves of change are looming, we must try to slow down our minds and hearts and think through the experiments we can design. The experiment process creates space for listening to God and paying attention to what God may be inviting us into in the midst of any given change in life. If change is constant, then so is the opportunity to experiment and, in so doing, embrace the experience God may have in mind for you throughout the change process.

16

MOVE YOUR MIND

*What mindset shifts are needed to
embrace life as an experiment?*

How can I live into God's future for me consistently?

My nephew, Amos, is an "I wanna see" kind of kid. If adults are talking about something, it's like a switch flips inside of him, and he drops what he is doing and says, "I wanna see!" He then proceeds to shove his six-year-old body in front of the cell phone you're looking at or climbs on a chair to see out the window at the contraption in the neighbor's yard we are commenting on. He is learning that the social contract typically suggests that one ask if they can see what you are holding in your hand rather than taking it abruptly. He is also learning that not everything adults talk about out the window is actually interesting enough to leave the show he is watching or the LEGO set he is building.

We can learn something important from kids like Amos: we need to move in order to see. From the beginning of this book, I've suggested that "discernment through movement" is the way to get where we hope to be—right in God's preferred vision for our lives. When we move, we have a new vantage point, and thus we see, physically or spiritually, what we couldn't when we remained stationary. Just like Amos will grow out of some of his curiosity when he realizes he has better things to do, most of us don't wake up wondering what God is doing every day. But what if that were true of us? What if the guiding questions for our lives were *What is God doing?* and *How can I join in?*

Our lives would be different. I think they would be infused with purpose and meaning. As I've led you through this process of experimenting and discussing the role discernment plays in your decision-making, I have been encouraging you to think differently but also to act differently. Psychologists have long debated whether thinking differently leads us to live differently or if living differently leads us to think differently. I'd say there is evidence that both are true. Mindset shifting is a concept that can be helpful for us all in various ways. For instance, if you have a "fixed mindset," then you are not as ready to learn as someone with a "growth mindset." However, if you began to pour yourself into learning something new that interested you, that action would have the potential to shift your mindset from fixed to growth.

CHANGE YOUR MIND, CHANGE YOUR LIFE—CHANGE YOUR LIFE, CHANGE YOUR MIND

The study of the human brain shows that changing our mindset can lead us to take actions we previously had avoided. Psychologist Alia Crum has studied the role of mindset in how we respond to challenges in life.[1] She and other psychologists have confirmed that chemicals are released differently in our brains when we approach something with anticipation rather than trepidation. The brain is capable of developing new neural pathways, even later in life. Maybe you've heard the concept of "brain plasticity," or this idea that the brain can still be molded and shaped as we learn and grow.[2] Kids and young people have brains that are very "plastic" and easily shaped. This is why we want to be careful what kids are exposed to as they grow. However, we now know that our brains can still be shaped long into adulthood. It may take more practice and repetition, but our minds can be transformed and shaped, and thus we can experience profound transformation at any season of life.

When the apostle Paul was writing to the church in Rome in the first century, he had no concept of brain chemistry or science like we do today, yet these profound words resonate with what we now know about how our minds are shaped and change: "I urge you, brothers and sisters, in view of God's mercy, to offer your bodies as a living sacrifice, holy and pleasing to God—this is your true and proper worship. Do not conform to the pattern of this world, but be transformed by the renewing of your mind. Then you will be able to test and approve what God's will is—his good, pleasing and perfect will."[3]

Notice that Paul is bringing up the very concept we've been exploring: actions lead to a change of mind, but a change of mind leads to a change of actions. He starts by inviting an action—give your whole life to God because of God's love and mercy for you. You can imagine the many actions that could accompany becoming a "living sacrifice." I love the way Eugene Peterson puts it in The Message translation: "So here's what I want you to do, God helping you: Take your everyday, ordinary life—your sleeping, eating, going-to-work, and walking-around life—and place it before God as an offering."[4]

Live out this faith even in the little things, your "walking-around life." But then Paul moves to the idea of changing your mindset. Don't just let your mind be conformed to the world around you, but intentionally change and transform your mind. As Paul describes it, this is not a one-time thing—renewing is a process that continues. I think about the little molds that come with some of the variety packs of Play-Doh. If our minds are as moldable as Play-Doh, will we just choose to shove the dough into the basic molds that come with the set? Will we just let our minds and hearts be shaped in the basic molds, the default patterns in the world around us? Or will we get creative, use our hands, and build all sorts of new shapes?

Think about what you see as the default in the cultures around you. While some aspects could be positive, the default molds usually look selfish and individualistic, as the world often shapes people to be arrogant and motivated by what is best for you and those like you. We live in a world that tells us we always need more stuff, and we need to look and act in certain ways to gain the fleeting approval of others. Realizing that the basic patterns around us are destructive helps us see why we should be transformed, but the renewing of our minds is not just about making sure God is happy with us or getting a pat on the back from Jesus. This is about the life that God wants for us because God loves us.

THE SHIFTS WE NEED TO MAKE

As we are rounding the corner to the conclusion of this process together, let's talk about the mindset shifts I've been inviting you to consider but also some practices that could help you "behave your way into new thinking," as I sometimes call it.

The first shift is from foolishness to wisdom. Now, I don't mean to offend anyone by calling you foolish, but I do think it would be helpful to expand our definition of foolishness. Most would define *foolishness* as making intentionally destructive decisions. But if foolishness is on the opposite side of the spectrum from wisdom, could there be more to it than that?

Proverbs is written as wisdom and advice given to the reader. In Proverbs 4:6–7, this is what is said of wisdom: "Do not forsake wisdom, and she will protect you; love her, and she will watch over you. The beginning of wisdom is this: Get wisdom. Though it cost all you have, get understanding." It's as though anything less than wisdom is foolishness. It almost seems foolish to follow this advice to get wisdom even though it may cost you everything! The truth is, foolishness doesn't only look like intentionally destructive behaviors. It can also look like settling for "good enough" or avoiding the decision you know deep down you need to discern. It can look like trying to let a pros-and-cons list or a strategic plan replace God's voice rather than starting with listening to God and merely including those tools along the way.

What would it look like to have the mindset of wisdom? Behave your way into new thinking by following the advice in James 1:5—to ask God for wisdom because God promises to give it to you. Make it a practice for a week to pray for wisdom from God three times a day. Put an alarm on your phone to remind you in the morning, midday, and evening.

The next shift is from fearing the future to choosing to see your life as an adventure of trust with God. To do this, we must let go of decisions with predetermined outcomes and embrace experiments with learning outcomes. This shift is the overarching goal of this book. We all want to make good decisions, but we are held back by the false idea that we can determine the outcomes of most decisions before we make them. This is why the practice of experimenting we've dug into in this book is so important.

What would it look like to commit to experimenting in a new way in your life? A practice you may want to choose is to think of one area of life—only one—and commit to a short, perhaps month-long experiment in that area. That will help you start to behave your way into new thinking. After years of thinking about discernment and decision-making this way, it's become almost a gut reaction for me to think through the mindset of experimenting. I not only believe the words from Ralph Waldo Emerson, "All of life is an experiment"—I live it![5] But that mindset didn't come naturally; it was the slow work of being transformed by the renewing of my mind. I've seen many of those whom I have coached move into this way of being, and I believe it can happen for you.

The next shift is from passive to active waiting. Quite often, when someone wants to step into a new direction in a job, or is finally ready to take finding a life partner seriously, or wants to take action on the dream they've had in their heart for a long time, they realize they can't make the move the way they thought they could. They realize they are in a season of waiting. But the mistake is to think that they cannot make any moves while in a time of waiting.

When it comes to seasons of waiting, I like to use an image of a sheep pasture. Imagine you're in one pasture, hoping to move on to the next, but the gate is locked. What are your options? Sure, you can lie down on the grass for a while—some time to rest is a great idea! But that's not all; you can explore the pasture you are in and make sure that before you are led to the next one, you have seen and learned all you can from the present one. Active waiting means seeing every moment and every season as having space to prepare for the next one we may be led into. What experiments can you do even in a time of waiting that can help you learn and grow in preparation for the space you are waiting to enter?

Finally, we need to shift from the desire to chart a perfect course to exploring the unknown. Perfectionism can derail us and hold us back from making even small decisions. We can be decisive and stop wavering when we throw off the idea that there is a map for the uncharted future God is leading us into. We can start thinking about small experiments that lead us to big decisions. This is so much better than needing to think ten steps ahead or hopelessly looking for a crystal ball to see around the mountain in front of us. This is not possible, especially since we live in a time when landmarks are changing and every map becomes outdated quickly. Cultural earthquakes have left the terrain looking nothing like the charts others have tried to follow. But rather than let this lead to anxiety, we can let it fill us with courage, because God has led God's people through uncharted space time and time again. God is always pointing us toward God's preferred future for us, and God's promise to be with us no matter what never fails.

My desire for you is that curiosity and wonder could lead the way as you follow God's Spirit into your future. I hope that as you make plans, as we all do, that you will also plan to be surprised by what God may have in store. My prayer is that your mind will be transformed and it will change the way you live. It will take intentionality, courage, and a trusted community, but it is possible to move into the future God has for you with confidence and anticipation.

17

THE END OF THE STORY

Who is the main character of the story?

Why keep the end of the story in mind?

I have seen every episode of the TV show *Friends*. I watched this fictional group of six friends become adults in New York City at the same time as I was becoming an adult myself. The show was incredibly popular for an audience of people from North American dominant culture who could see themselves in the story. The show didn't represent everyone, and it certainly had its problematic elements, but I could see my own story within the story of these friends. While I couldn't understand how they could afford those apartments in the city, the things they struggled with and the quirky situations they found themselves in gave me a sense that they could be my actual friends.

In 2020, *Friends* was taken off of Netflix and moved to HBO. Instead of purchasing yet another streaming subscription, I decided to try to watch some of the episodes one last time. I'm sure many people were rewatching them! I realized quickly that I was never going to have time to rewatch them all. I had a lot more free time decades ago, when the show first aired. So in the last week before it was removed, I found myself drawn to watching the last few episodes of the show. The finale (spoiler alert!) brings together all ten years of storytelling in a masterful way.

But if you hadn't watched the other episodes, the ending wouldn't make much sense. You wouldn't know why Joey buys a little chick and a baby duck as a housewarming gift for Monica and Chandler. If you had skipped to the ending, you would be confused about why it is such a big deal that Ross ends up with Rachel and why the very worst thing that Ross could say during their embrace and commitment to be together forever is "unless we are on a break." But he says it—and you would know that's typical because Ross is always putting his foot in his mouth!

Some of you are probably smiling at the memories of these episodes, but if not, think of a TV show or series of movies or books that you have read every word or seen every minute of. No matter what story you are thinking of, *the end of the story is most meaningful when you've experienced the fullness of the story leading up to it.* We are not characters in *Friends*, they are not real people, and they are not my real friends . . . Sorry, just a quick reminder for myself.

But we are characters in what many would suggest is the greatest, deepest, most profound story that has ever been told: the story God is writing, in which we are invited to participate. And just like watching the last episode of *Friends* or the last movie in the *Lord of the Rings* series, we can see how it turns out in the end. In the end of God's story, God restores all of creation in what is referred to in Scripture as the New Heavens and the New Earth.[1] All the wrong things are made right, so there is no more death, crying, or pain. Jesus declares, "I am making everything new!" We see in that final episode that people from every "tongue, tribe and nation" are singing to God together with one voice, but still all in their own languages—an incredible image of unity in diversity.[2]

Earlier in the book, we looked back at the four acts of this cosmic play that have led up to today. Now we are in the middle of act 5, and we don't have a script—but we do know how it ends. If we are going to be ready to appreciate all the fullness of that grand finale, then we need to experience the fullness of the story leading up to it.

This is Jesus's invitation to us, to experience the full life that he talked about while walking the earth.[3] When we experience this life in all its fullness, we will be making improvisational decisions that line up with the end of the story. God is the main character, and that's why the grand finale shows Jesus at the center of it all, but as supporting characters, we have an incredible role to play. If we know that the end is unity in diversity, then we pursue unity with all we have, one improv move at a time, because there is no script for how to do this. If we know the end is all wrong things being made right, we join God now in making things right by looking for what God is doing and following the Spirit's lead. If we know the end is free from pain, then in our current suffering, we receive what that trial can teach us in our lives to shape us for the future, where we are free from it all.

To embrace the fullness of life God wants to lead us into, we will have to surrender perfectionism, apathy, fear, or whatever holds us back from making a move. That surrender won't be a one-time thing but a regular part of the process. Join in the long line of people trying to follow God's Spirit through the ages, one experiment at a time. They may have used different language for it, and perhaps you will too. But whatever you do, create space in your process to listen to God, however you experience God's voice in your life. Find the people who can process the complexity of life's most overwhelming choices with you. Break down those daunting decisions into steps that help you learn more as you choose to take action on them. Then take your learning and apply it to the next experiment and the next as you find yourself discerning God's leadership in your life by making one move and then another.

When you find yourself feeling stuck or stalled, remember these words from Ralph Waldo Emerson: "Do not be too timid and squeamish about your actions. All life is an experiment. The more experiments you make, the better."[4]

ACKNOWLEDGMENTS

It takes a whole team to keep me going in life. I have no problem admitting that I need a lot of help to stay a healthy person and leader. The same folks who help me stay grounded and supported in life are those who have made this book possible. First of all, to my husband, JD, your hard work in taking care of so much for our family is why I am able to write in my free time. I love you, and I'm incredibly grateful for you!

The topic of this book and the theology it's grounded in is core to my life and work. My colleague Dr. Michael Binder helped me engage the topic of listening and responding to God in ways that I never had before we met thirteen years ago. Many deep conversations over the years of leading a church together have taken a theology and made it practical. Thank you, Michael, for the many years of collaboration and friendship. Thank you to my staff at Mill City Church—there is no way this book would have been written during this pandemic if you weren't such rockstars!

Thank you to my ride-or-die Jo for all of the support and challenges over the years. Without your influence in my life, I wouldn't be an author. Thank you to my spiritual director, Jean, for teaching me what discernment truly looks like over the last thirteen years. Thank you to my family and to my friends who basically are family. Thanks to Anna for being my muse and sounding board. Thank you to Christine for continuing to generously offer me space to write. Thank you to my agent, Rachelle; my editor, Lisa; and the team at Broadleaf Books.

Thank you to the many people who have helped me make decisions over the years—my friends, family, therapists, and mentors. Thank you to those who have been in my discipleship groups and teams and members of my Mill City Church community for being the guinea pigs who helped me determine how to live out this way of discerning God's movement in the world in practical ways. You inspire me, and because of all of you, I get up every day motivated to live a life worth imitating. You are why this book exists!

Above all, I am thankful to the Spirit of Jesus. How incredible that the triune God saw it fit to come to us in the form of a counselor and guide—your empowerment is the reason my goal every day is to try to follow your lead in this disorienting world.

APPENDIX

DECISION-MAKING TOOLBOX

This toolbox includes simple tools to help you make decisions. Different tools will work better for different decisions. Read through the various tools and apply the one that seems most helpful for the decision you are facing.

Go to PastorSteph.com/makeamove for a downloadable version of this toolbox and corresponding worksheets.

LOSING MY MARBLES: HOW SURE IS SURE?

This tool is part of one of the case studies for chapter 11 about vocational experiments. When it comes to making decisions, we often struggle with just how sure we need to be to make the final decision. Because 100 percent certainty isn't an option, you must ask yourself, What level of assurance do I need to feel in order to make a move? We can easily flip-flop, going from yes one day to no the next depending on our feelings that day, the conversations we had, and so on. Here is a practical and tangible way to move forward:

Step 1: Find or buy a mason jar (or another clear container) and one hundred marbles.

Step 2: Determine what your percentage of certainty must be in order to make this decision.

Step 3: If you've decided it's 80 percent, then count out and remove twenty marbles; if it's 70 percent, remove thirty; and so on. Put them aside in a drawer.

Step 4: Put a bowl next to the jar. In the jar, place the number of marbles that represent how sure you are about the decision at that moment. Talk with a friend if you need help gauging the amount. Place the remaining marbles in the bowl next to the jar.

Step 5: Over the next few weeks, as you talk with friends and family, spend time in prayer, and think through the logistics of the decision, consider the marbles. After each day, reflect on the process and add marbles to the jar for experiences that increased your assurance or take some out and put them in the bowl if you felt your experiences decreased your assurance.

Step 6: Give yourself a deadline and tell a friend that you plan to decide by that day.

FEEDBACK RUBRIC: NOT ALL FEEDBACK IS CREATED EQUAL

When it comes to making life decisions, the opinions of others inevitably impact our discernment. In most decisions, it is important that others weigh in. See the Clearness Committee tool for a structured way to receive feedback. Our friends and family members will share their opinions throughout our regular conversations and interactions. But if we aren't intentional, we may give too much weight to one person's opinion and not enough to another's. When we give feedback from others the appropriate weight based on these factors, then that feedback can be critical in helping us make a move.

Get out a sheet of paper and turn it sideways so you can make four long lines from the left to the right, representing four spectrums. Put a minus sign on the left side of the paper and a plus sign on the right. On the left side of the page, label each of the four spectrums as follows:

1. Kind of Feedback
2. Kind of Person
3. Clarity of Feedback
4. Relevance to Context

Now consider a piece of feedback you have received and circle where on each spectrum the feedback fits. The minus sign represents putting little or low weight on the feedback, and as you move closer to the plus sign, it represents high or significant weight to this feedback. Use the following steps for each spectrum.

Kind of Feedback

You are not evaluating whether someone critiqued or affirmed you here. Rather, you are evaluating the way the feedback is delivered, which is more important as we judge the weight to put on the specific feedback.

An explicit accusation would land on the lowest end of the spectrum and a passive-aggressive comment a bit to the right. In the middle would be neutral or generally affirming comments.

A specific compliment or a constructive critique would move toward a heavier weight. Perhaps the most significant weight would be put on a positive challenge that affirms who you are but also challenges you to grow or go farther.

Kind of Person

Who is giving the feedback is nearly as important as the feedback itself. This spectrum can help you determine how much weight to give feedback based on the kind of person offering that feedback.

On the low end of the spectrum is an enemy or a "hater." Though it can be hard, you must not give much weight to the opinions of those who do not have your best interests in mind. Unhealthy friends and family members would still be low on the spectrum. It's difficult to realize that those you love are not always in a place to give you helpful feedback because of their personal struggles. A knowledgeable acquaintance would be in the middle of the spectrum, followed by healthy family members or friends. The highest weight can be given to trusted experts in this area or a mentor who has your best interests in mind.

Clarity of Feedback

When feedback is unclear, it is unhelpful, but when it is clear and direct, it can be gold! This spectrum can help you determine how much weight to give feedback based on its clarity.

On the low end of the spectrum is inaccurate information; next would be unclear or confusing information. In the middle are exaggerated statements or generalizations. Even if the feedback is positive, it's wise to avoid giving significant weight to feedback that isn't clear or is hyperbolic. Specific feedback that can help you think through its application should be given the most weight.

Relevance to Context

Some feedback is irrelevant to the context in which you want to apply it. People often give feedback that doesn't fit the context in which you are trying to grow, and giving that feedback too much weight can confuse you as you try to make decisions. This spectrum can help you determine the weight you should give feedback based on its relevance.

On the low end of the spectrum is completely irrelevant feedback, followed by feedback whose relevance is unclear. In the middle is potentially or partially relevant feedback. More weight should be given to feedback that applies to the context and is highly relevant to the current realities you are facing.

After you mark the significance of the feedback on each of the four spectrums, you will have an idea of how much weight you should give to various pieces of feedback that you receive throughout your discernment process.

THE FOUR TENS

This is an adaptation of a tool created by business writer Suzy Welch that has come to be known as the 10-10-10 rule. I like to add an additional "10," so that's why I call it "The Four Tens." Imagine that you've hypothetically chosen one of your options. Now think through the following questions:

- How will I feel about it ten minutes from now?
- How about ten weeks from now?
- How about ten months from now?
- How about ten years from now?

After trying to imagine how you would feel, now ask the same four questions, but this time, imagine that Jesus is there with you in the room. Imagine Jesus there with you ten minutes from now. What is his posture? What do you imagine he may say or do? Now ten weeks, ten months, and ten years—imagine Jesus is there with you and what his reaction may be.

CLEARNESS COMMITTEE: WHO ARE YOUR PEOPLE?

Many groups within our faith tradition have held up the value of community discernment and listening to God together. The Catholic Jesuit tradition calls this practice "communal discernment," modeled after church father Ignatius of Loyola. Others in the contemplative tradition have "spiritual direction groups" that meet regularly. In the 1600s, the Quaker tradition developed what was later termed "clearness committees," acknowledging just how hard it can be to discern how God is leading us and showing us why we need others to help bring clarity, or clearness.

Spiritual writer and activist Parker Palmer has written about the clearness committee concept.[1] Based on his writings, I've developed a simple outline to help guide a clearness committee (see chapter 5). Here are some questions you can use as you follow that outline with your own clearness committee:

What do you hear when you pray and listen to God?

What emotions do you experience when you think or pray about this decision?

What is the dynamic between you and others whom this decision impacts?

What have others you trust in your life said about this decision?

If Jesus were here physically right now, how do you imagine he would respond to you as you face this decision?

Imagine each decision you could make: What emotions do you have as you imagine each scenario?

For more great resources on the idea of a clearness committee and the "Circle of Trust" method designed by Palmer and his organization, the Center for Courage and Renewal, head to CourageRenewal.org.

WORTH THE RISK: RISK ASSESSMENT

Everyone has a different tolerance for risk. When it comes to making decisions, it can be helpful to perform a risk assessment. Here is a short example of a general risk assessment that could apply to many decisions. You can add up your score below.

How much is at stake for your emotional and physical health and well-being?

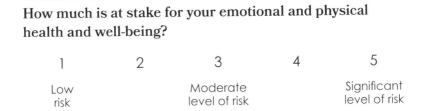

1	2	3	4	5
Low risk		Moderate level of risk		Significant level of risk

How much is at stake for your financial health and resources?

1	2	3	4	5
Low risk		Moderate level of risk		Significant level of risk

How would this affect your relationships with those close to you or the situation?

1	2	3	4	5
Little change		Moderate change		Significant change

How will this affect your calendar? What will you have to adjust?

1	2	3	4	5
Little change		Moderate change		Significant change

How many other aspects of life will you need to adjust if you make this decision?

1	2	3	4	5
Little change		Moderate change		Significant change

How big of a learning curve will there be if you make this decision?

1	2	3	4	5
Mild curve		Moderate curve		Significant curve

If you decide not to make this decision, will you miss out on ways that you could otherwise grow and learn?

1	2	3	4	5
Significant growth		Moderate growth		No growth

If you decide not to make this decision, will you miss out on potential opportunities?

1	2	3	4	5
Low risk		Moderate level of risk		Significant level of risk

30–40 Significant Risk: Be cautious as you move forward. Sometimes high-risk decisions are still good decisions, but make sure you do some lower-risk experimenting if possible. It is critical to bring in wise counsel as you consider this decision.

20–29 High Risk: Many important decisions in life are on the risky end of the spectrum. The fact that they are risky is part of why they are important. Examine each area you marked as a high number and consider the ramifications of your decision before you move forward. Bring those you trust into the discussion regarding high-risk decisions.

10–19 Moderate Risk: You can often make these decisions by thinking them through or talking them out with a trusted conversation partner. However, pay attention to which areas you marked as high risk.

5–9 Low Risk: Low-risk decisions can still be important, but the low-risk designation can help you avoid the trap of letting a low-risk decision cause high levels of stress.

THE WELL-BEING WHEEL: DECISIONS THAT ARE GOOD FOR YOU

When it comes to making good decisions, we need to remember that we are whole people. Decisions need to be good for you—*all* of who you are. Our holistic well-being will depend on making sure the decisions we make are good for all aspects of our lives. My friend Dr. Christine Osgood developed the Well-Being Wheel for the Center of Wellbeing at Bethel University. She would say the wheel is "designed to remind you of six foundational aspects of life that influence your intrapersonal wellbeing."

Here are the six aspects of the Well-Being Wheel described by Dr. Osgood:

1. *The Spiritual Dimension.* Your spirit is the part of you that can sense, communicate, and interconnect with our transcendent God. This is the part of you that notices the promptings of the Holy Spirit, the part of you that desires to be like Jesus.
2. *The Cognitive Dimension.* Your "mind" has a cognitive side and an emotional side. The cognitive side of the "mind coin" refers to your thoughts and thinking processes and also includes your memory and imagination.
3. *The Relational Dimension.* You are a social being. You were designed for connection with other humans. You have been shaped by the social context you grew up in and were socially conditioned to relate with other humans in certain ways.
4. *The Meaning Dimension.* Your sense of meaning and purpose for life influences your intrapersonal well-being. Specifically, once you identify why you exist, you begin to make choices and exert your will to make certain things happen

in life. Your will aligns your life with your sense of meaning and purpose.

5. *The Physical Dimension.* This dimension focuses on caring for various biological systems in the human body because of how these systems influence your cognition and mood.

6. *The Emotional Dimension.* Your emotions are the other side of the "mind coin." Your emotions are a mix of physiological experiences and cognitive appraisals. Each person needs to become savvy at identifying, navigating, and managing their emotions.

When you are making an important decision, take time going through each of the six aspects and think about how the different options would affect each area of your life. If you can journal your thoughts, that could help you assess the different dimensions of your well-being. It could also be helpful to process your reflections with a conversation partner.

To see a visual of this wheel, head to https://www.wellbeing-at -bethel.com.

NOTES

CHAPTER 1

1 Eva M. Krockow, "How Many Decisions Do We Make Each Day?," *Psychology Today*, September 27, 2018, https://tinyurl.com/yy8l9koe.

2 John 14:1–31.

3 Acts 15:28.

4 John 14:6.

5 John 10:10.

6 Ruth Haley Barton, *Pursuing God's Will Together* (Downers Grove, IL: InterVarsity, 2012), 20.

CHAPTER 2

1 Acts 16:6–15.

2 Acts 16:7.

3 Jo Saxton, *More Than Enchanting* (Downers Grove, IL: InterVarsity, 2012), 49.

CHAPTER 3

1 Scot Thomas, "The 12 Steps of Alcoholics Anonymous (AA)," Alcohol.org, https://www.alcohol.org/alcoholics-anonymous/.

CHAPTER 4

1 Matt 11:5; 15:13–14; 23:16–19; Luke 4:18; 6:39–42; John 9:35–41.
2 Matt 9:27–34; 20:30; Mark 8:22–26; 10:46–52; Luke 18:35; John 9:1–12.
3 John 8:12.
4 John 9:39.
5 Acts 9:1–19.
6 Mark 5:36; Luke 8:50.
7 John 16:31.
8 John 4:48.
9 Mark 9:24.
10 Mike Breen, *Building a Discipling Culture* (Pawleys Island, SC: 3DM, 2011), 76. This book was fundamental in my journey of learning how to listen and respond to God. If you are looking for a way to process with a group of people what it looks like to do this discernment in a discipleship group model, I highly recommend this resource.
11 Monica Gagliano, Mavra Grimonprez, Martial Depczynski, and Michael Renton, "Tuned In: Plant Roots Use Sound to Locate Water," *Oecologia* 184 (2017): 151–160, https://tinyurl.com/y6rhpcpx.
12 John 4:10–14 (paraphrase).

CHAPTER 5

1 James 1:5.
2 Parker J. Palmer, "The Clearness Committee," Center for Courage & Renewal, accessed May 24, 2020, https://tinyurl .com/y4wreogr.
3 Palmer, "Clearness Committee."

CHAPTER 6

1 John Carpenter, "Boston Beer Company's Jim Koch on the Crucial Difference between Dangerous and Merely Scary," *Forbes*, May 31, 2016, https://tinyurl.com/y7xnjfyw.

CHAPTER 7

1 Tina Fey, *Bossypants* (New York: Reagan Arthur Books, 2011), 76.
2 N. T. Wright, *The New Testament and the People of God* (Minneapolis: Fortress Press, 1992), 140.
3 There is so much written on what we call the metanarrative, and N. T. Wright's work is a great starting place if this is intriguing to you.
4 N. T. Wright, *Scripture and the Authority of God: How to Read the Bible Today* (New York: HarperOne, 2011), 123.
5 Jeremiah 6:16.

CHAPTER 8

1 Meg Jay, *The Defining Decade* (New York: Twelve, 2013), xxvi.
2 Jay, *Defining Decade*, 35.
3 Stanford d.school website, accessed May 24, 2020, https://dschool.stanford.edu/.
4 "About Stanford d.school," Stanford d.school website, accessed May 24, 2020, https://tinyurl.com/y4vp2nvs.
5 Stanford d.school website.
6 Stanford d.school website.

CHAPTER 9

1 Scott Reall, *Journey to Freedom* (Nashville: Thomas Nelson, 2008).
2 Psalm 27:8–9.
3 Psalm 42:5.
4 Proverbs 11:14; 15:22; 24:6.
5 Gary Thomas, *Sacred Pathways* (Grand Rapids: Zondervan, 1996).

CHAPTER 10

1 See Daniel J. Siegel, *No Drama Discipline* (New York: Bantam Books, 2016).
2 World Vision, "Our Water Work," accessed September 25, 2020, https://tinyurl.com/y68su8m2.
3 Hebrews 12:1 MSG.
4 Frederick Buechner, *Wishful Thinking* (New York: HarperOne, 1993), 118.

5 To learn more about the clean water crisis and how you can help the way Jordan did in the case study, head to www.fieldsoflife.org.

CHAPTER 11

1 Micaela di Leonardo, "The Female World of Cards and Holidays: Women, Families, and the Work of Kinship," *Signs* 12, no. 3 (1987): 440–453, https://tinyurl.com/yytwsu3l.
2 Genesis 1:27.
3 Chip Heath and Dan Heath, "The 10/10/10 Rule for Tough Decisions," *Fast Company*, April 1, 2013, https://tinyurl.com/yy9bv2ce.

CHAPTER 12

1 Shauna Niequist, Facebook, June 3, 2014, https://tinyurl.com/y63fmlgt.
2 Rose Coser, *In Defense of Modernity* (Stanford: Stanford University Press, 1991); Ethan Waters, *Urban Tribes* (London: Bloomsbury, 2004).

CHAPTER 13

1 John 10:10.
2 Emily P. Freeman, *The Next Right Thing* (Grand Rapids: Baker, 2019), 17–18.

3 John H. Walton, Mark Chavalas, and Victor Harold Matthews, *The IVP Bible Background Commentary: Old Testament* (Downers Grove, IL: InterVarsity, 2000), 88.

4 Mike Breen, *Oikonomics* (Pawleys Island, SC: 3DM, 2014).

CHAPTER 14

1 Isaiah 43:1–3a.

2 Isaiah 43:18–21.

3 *Merriam-Webster.com Dictionary*, s.v. "disillusion," accessed July 20, 2020, https://www.merriam-webster.com/dictionary/disillusion.

CHAPTER 15

1 "Heraclitus," *Stanford Encyclopedia of Philosophy*, updated September 3, 2019, https://tinyurl.com/y2edscpz.

2 Anatole France, *The Crime of Sylvestre Bonnard* (Garden City: Harper and Brothers, 1890).

CHAPTER 16

1 Alia J. Crum, Modupe Akinola, Ashley Martin, and Sean Fath, "The Role of Stress Mindset in Shaping Cognitive, Emotional, and Physiological Responses to Challenging and Threatening Stress," *Anxiety, Stress, & Coping* 30, no. 4 (2017): 379–395, https://tinyurl.com/y4py5vu5.

2 Bryan Kolb, Robbin Gibb, and Terry Robinson, "Brain Plasticity and Behavior," Association for Psychological Science, https://tinyurl.com/y3zpweum.

3 Romans 12:1–2.

4 Romans 12:1–2 MSG.

5 Ralph Waldo Emerson, *Journals of Ralph Waldo Emerson, with Annotations—1841–1844* (Cambridge: Riverside, 1913).

CHAPTER 17

1 Revelation 21:1–4.

2 Revelation 7:9–10.

3 John 10:10.

4 Ralph Waldo Emerson, *Journals of Ralph Waldo Emerson, with Annotations—1841–1844* (Cambridge: Riverside, 1913).

APPENDIX

1 Palmer, "Clearness Committee."